The Word of a Gentleman

Meditations for Modern Man

Also by Dr. Halverson . . .
Man to Man
Be Yourself—and God's
Perspective
The Quiet Man
Manhood With Meaning
Between Sundays
A Day at a Time

The Word of a Gentleman

Meditations for Modern Man

Richard C. Halverson

Zondervan Publishing House
Grand Rapids, Michigan

To faithful Christian laymen
who with silent heroism under relentless secular pressure
fight the economic battle as stewards of the living God
and whose faithful stewardship
honors Jesus Christ our Lord
as it promotes the work of His kingdom.
Thank God upon every remembrance of these faithful men.

THE WORD OF A GENTLEMAN
Copyright © 1983 by The Zondervan Corporation
Grand Rapids, Michigan

This book was formerly published under the title *Perspective.* Copyright 1957 by
Cowman Publishing Company.

Daybreak Books are published by Zondervan Publishing House,
1415 Lake Drive, S.E., Grand Rapids, Michigan 49506

Library of Congress Cataloging in Publication Data

Halverson, Richard C.
    The word of a gentleman.

        Rev. ed. of: Perspective. 1957.
        1. Men—Prayer-books and devotions—English.
    I. Halverson, Richard C. Perspective. II. Title.
    BV4843.H34   1983   242'.642   83-23598
    ISBN 0-310-25811-1

Printed in the United States of America

86   87   88   89   90 / 22   21   20   19   18   17

Contents

The Word of a Gentleman

Meditations for Modern Man

Perspective

A certain man had been having difficulty with discouragement and depression resulting in some physical disability. He consulted a physician.

The first question the doctor asked him was, "Do you have a view in your home?"

At first it might seem there is little if any connection between a view and depression or dyspepsia. But as a matter of fact there is!

Perspective makes all the difference in the world to a man. Sometimes a long look at life is the best medicine.

In the midst of nervous tension and discouragement, stop to ask yourself this question some time, "One year from now how important will this thing be that is bothering me so much?"

A man gets so bottled up with little problems that if he doesn't try to see beyond them they can suffocate him.

Someone has put it this way: "It is worse to be nibbled to death by minnows than to be swallowed by a whale." Little things can pick away at a man until they wear him down to nothing.

Little things can ruin a man's day unless he learns the art of looking away—far enough away and beyond them to get a perspective.

This is one of the basic values of a quiet time every day. It lifts a person out of the details that smother him—lets him breathe—get a new slant on things—a clear view.

One business executive, when asked the secret of his success, replied immediately: "The one thing which has helped me most in my business has been the practice I've followed for twenty-five years of spending the first thirty minutes undisturbed in my office in prayer, Bible reading, and meditation."

Nothing was allowed to interfere with these first golden minutes of each day when he was "alone with God." They made it possible for him to face the day's responsibilities and decisions with a maximum of efficiency—a minimum of fuss. He had the long look. He had a view!

One professional man took the first thirty minutes after lunch for his quiet time. Behind closed doors (no telephones) he would open his Bible and read a portion—then drop to his knees beside his desk for a time of prayer. After which he would rise, sit in his chair, turn and face the window at his back, and look out over the city for five or ten minutes. *He got his view!*

In addition to the spiritual nourishment and strength the quiet time gives, it helps a man take the long look. It makes him the master of his circumstances instead of the victim of them.

The man who takes time with God daily is way ahead!

"They that wait for the LORD shall renew their strength . . ." (Isa. 40:31).

Leadership Is a Mission Field

Leadership too is a mission field!

In fact, in a sense it is a most difficult mission field. Perhaps that is why it has been neglected. The man who has risen to leadership doesn't convince easily—isn't overwhelmed by facts—is hard to get to sometimes.

Of course there are solid—dependable—faithful Christian leaders in government, business, industry, labor, education, and the professions . . . but there are also many who are not Christian—who do not know the first thing about authentic Christianity!

The average in leadership is probably about the same as the average in any other category: Some are genuinely Christian. Others are nominally Christian. Many are utterly indifferent.

Nominal Christians are a mission field also! They are not vocal for righteousness. It is bad enough when any Christian (so-called) fails to be articulate for Christ and righteousness . . . but infinitely worse when a leader fails. . .

Because the higher a man stands in leadership—the wider the radius of his influence—good or ill!

A man's influence works in two ways: Positively or negatively . . . never neutrally! The man who doesn't take a stand for Christ in leadership is taking a stand against Him in the very nature of the case.

Indifference toward Christ by the man at the top filters down and around infecting those around him and below him. This is inevitable! Many young men in an organization remain indifferent to Christ because they see nothing in their leaders to inspire interest.

Not that their leaders are evil men. On the contrary! The fact that they are good men who seem to get along without Christ and His church feeds the younger man's indifference. What's good enough for "the boss" is good enough for him.

If the man at the top can get along without taking Christ seriously . . . why should the ambitious young man down the line bother?

Who can measure the incalculable loss resulting from the spiritual indifference of some leadership? Leadership too is a mission field!

"Everyone who acknowledges me before men, I also will

acknowledge before my Father who is in heaven; but whoever denies me before men, I also will deny before my Father who is in heaven"—Jesus Christ as recorded in Matthew 10:32–33.

True Greatness. . .

"Peter went out and wept. . . . "

That was the beginning of real manhood for Peter! The manhood was there before—it had been built into him at birth, but it needed to be discovered . . . needed to be released from the false pride under which it was buried.

Up to this time Peter was filled with self-sufficiency. He was used to throwing his weight around. The other fishermen respected him—kept their distance. He was strong—outspoken—a born leader . . . but he needed to be broken!

(Like a good horse, a good man needs to be broken before he's really useful.)

A few hours earlier Peter had boasted to Jesus, "Though all men forsake thee, I will never forsake thee." The Lord responded by telling Peter he would deny Him three times before the cock crowed.

But Peter boasted more vociferously: "Though they kill me I will never forsake thee!"

In a matter of hours Peter let the accusation of a little serving girl frighten him into denying Jesus with a curse. "I don't know the man!" Peter blasted profanely.

Then the cock crowed—Peter remembered what Jesus had said and he went out and wept . . . a broken man!

That was the beginning of *true greatness* in Peter!

Now he began to see himself as God saw him. He began to

see his weakness—his pride—his false strength—his bull-headedness—his outspokenness. He was rocked by the realization that he was everything his given name "Simon" implied.

Simon means "weak," "fickle" . . . Jesus had called him a "rock" (Peter). The thing he needed to learn, however, was that *only Jesus could make a Peter out of a Simon.* Only Jesus can make a rock out of a fickle, vacillating, boastful man.

True greatness comes this way—by the road of brokenness! No man is really great who has not been broken before God.

Until a man comes to the end of himself—until he reaches his extremity—becomes aware of his limitations . . . until he weeps over his own failure, he may be cocky and loud and bullish, but never great!

Peter learned to depend completely on God. He learned that he could be a man only when he humbled himself before God and bowed to the reign and rule of God in his life.

The strongest men in the world are those who are weak before God! The greatest men are those who are humble before God. The tallest men are those who bend before God.

This is the basic paradox of life: A man's greatness lies in his weakness. When *self-sufficiency* turns into *Christ-confidence,* a man is ready for anything!

Faith, Not Feeling

Do you fly "by the seat of your pants?"

Air Force jargon of course . . . but it's a serious matter. Many good pilots have "washed out" because they couldn't learn to trust their instruments when they disagreed with their feelings.

Plenty others have cracked up—victims of vertigo—because in the pinch they yielded to their "feel" and disregarded their instruments.

Men crack up spiritually too (if they ever get off the ground) because they cannot seem to learn to trust the promises of God instead of their feelings.

Some men never learn to fly, spiritually speaking, because they are victims of their feelings. They never learn to depend on God's Word.

What a catastrophe: good men washed up—grounded—when the promises of God are so utterly dependable—so utterly trustworthy. *They never fail!*

A major weakness among Christian men is that many confuse faith with feeling. They think they trust God when actually they trust only how they feel. And this becomes apparent in the pinches: life tumbles in—they feel lousy . . . and you'd think God could no longer be trusted.

As though God's promises are valid only when a man feels right!

Such men fly spiritually "by the seat of their pants." Everything depends on their feelings. Decisions are made and jobs are done in terms of feelings. Feel bad . . . nothing's accomplished—or a crackup—either one!

Circumstances crowd in like a fog—discouragement follows . . . and instead of trusting God's Word, the man yields to the vertigo of despair. *Crash!*

The wise flyer depends on his instruments no matter how radically they disagree with his "feel." *He obeys his instruments.*

Those instruments work just as well when ceiling is zero—visibility is zero—as they do in the clear. They are as trustworthy in storm and tempest as in fair weather. They'll bring a man in when weather looks impossible. In fact, when storms take over, the instruments are indispensable.

So does God's Word stand! Impregnable and invulnerable—invincible and exchangeable. A man can trust it implicitly—put his whole weight and the weight of his burden down on it. *It holds!*

Faith centers in God's faithfulness—not man's feeling. Faith is rooted and grounded in God's Word—not in man's instincts.

A man trusts God with his will, not his emotions. God is faithful. His promises are true. He can be depended on! That's a fact! Regardless of how a man feels, he does not allow his feelings to make a liar of God!

"All things are possible to him who believes" (Mark 9:23).

Spiritual Economics

The law of supply and demand works in the realm of the spirit too!

It's not a question of resources because the supply is inexhaustible. God's grace is limitless. He is never embarrassed by any lack. Nor is there ever a question of availability. God is not reluctant to give and bless and help.

As a matter of fact, not only is God not reluctant, but He has actually taken the initiative in blessing man. God is always on the offensive—always aggressive. The man who does not receive from God, won't! It is not a problem of supply.

Nor is it a question of demand. The world is filled with need. The consumer potential for God's resources is every-

17

where, all the time. Wherever one looks he sees a desperate need for that which only God has to offer.

Men do not always recognize this need . . . and often, though they recognize it, they are not willing to admit it. But even this is not the basic problem.

It's not a question of supply. It's not a question of demand. The real problem is *distribution!*

The question is how to bring God's supply and man's need together.

And the Christian man is the key! For in His divine economy God has chosen to bless through men who are available as channels. *God's method is men!*

When God wants to bless an individual—or an office—or a club—or a community—or a nation—or the world, He seeks a man to be the channel.

God uses men to bless men. The only thing that ever limits God's blessing is either man's unwillingness to be blessed, or the unavailability of Christian men to be used as the means whereby God directs the flow of blessing to the point of need.

This is not to say that God *could* not do it another way. But He *does* not! This is God's way in the world.

Every Christian man is where he is because God wants to use him there as a point of distribution. He's where he is because he has been placed there by God as a contact—the meeting place of God's supply and man's need.

"Never allow the thought 'I am of no use where I am.' You certainly are of no use where you are not!" (Oswald Chambers).

God wants to bless men through your life. Right where you live and work and play and socialize. He wants to work through you, but He can do this only if you are willing to be available—willing to yield your life to Him as a channel.

"Now unto Him Who is able to do exceedingly abundantly

above all that we ask or think . . . according to the power that worketh in us!" (Eph. 3:20).

Fitness Within

As a man's body craves health—his soul craves holiness!

Physical well-being: the sense of fitness—tone—strength—drive—hardness—is of immeasurable advantage whatever a man's work. To be in top shape spiritually is an infinitely greater advantage!

Good physical condition increases a man's efficiency and being "in condition" spiritually guarantees a man's best!

Holiness is not piety—or religiousness—or mysticism—or some other human imitation that so horribly misrepresents it. These human efforts at holiness are a tragic caricature of the real thing!

And they are usually repugnant to a normal man. Because every effort of man to make himself "holy" leads to self-righteousness and pride and hypocrisy.

Which explains why so many good people will have nothing to do with religion. They have been driven from it by those who have a false righteousness: those who are so heavenly minded, they are no earthly good!

True holiness is spiritual tone—fitness—strength—drive—sharpness. It means to be in shape within. It means inner resources and adequate reserve.

In fact, holiness is simply *spiritual health!*

It is attractive—desirable—magnetic. As men admire the star athlete, so they admire true holiness . . . *when they see it!*

19

Holiness is Christ-likeness! Nobody ever went wrong being like Jesus Christ! There is nothing superficial or weak or stuffy about Him!

If He should appear in the flesh in the average office or private club, men would be drawn to Him like bees to honey. There would be a quality about Him that would make Him the center of attraction.

Of course He'd have His enemies! Great men always have enemies. *Holiness will always draw opposition.* A man's enemies are often the most accurate index to the man. ("Beware when all men speak well of you.")

But good men—true men would be drawn to Him. Because He would demonstrate that which all men lack—even though they may not realize it. His life would reflect that which every man really wants deep down in his heart. His life would make us aware of the emptiness and corruption of our own.

As the aroma of good food whets the appetite, so the presence of Jesus Christ would awaken our desire for holiness, for spiritual wholeness!

Holiness is the gift of God! It cannot be earned. It is not achieved by effort. It can only be received. Christ purchased it by His sacrifice on the cross. It is not cheap—it is the costliest gift ever offered—but it is free!

"He who through faith is righteous shall live" (Rom. 1:17).

Eligibility

"I had no objection to God . . . but I didn't believe it was cricket to turn the mess that was me over to Him!"

Those are the words of a man who was a total failure at forty-three.

He had made a complete ruin of his life, and though he knew he needed God, he felt he had no right to turn to God in his extremity.

He had completely misjudged Christianity. He was victim of the very common (but very mistaken) view that God is a stern judge who is utterly irreconcilable to man's failure.

He had the idea that no man can come to God until he has earned the right . . . until his life somehow adds up . . . until he has achieved some nebulous standard of righteousness.

In the back of his mind he probably thought the church was for men who had reached perfection and therefore had some special right to God's favor. Obviously he didn't qualify. He didn't belong.

What he failed to realize is that *the church is for men who need God's grace*—not men who have earned it! Most sincere Christians are in church—not because they are sinless—but because they know they are sinners!

As the hospital to the sick, so the church is to men in need. A man doesn't wait until he is well to go to the hospital. The sicker he is, the greater his need of it. The sicker he is, the more he qualifies.

As it is the sick who are eligible for the hospital, so it is the sinner—the failure—who needs the church.

In fact, Jesus Himself made it clear that He was unable to help the religious people of His day . . . not because they did not need help, but because they refused to admit their need. In their self-righteousness they rejected His grace.

He said to them, "Those who are well have no need of a physician, but those who are sick. I have not come to call the righteous, but sinners to repentance" (Luke 5:31–32).

This is grace: unmerited favor. God helps the man who is not worthy of His help. God helps the weak man . . . and the weaker the man, the more eligible he is for God's help. This is grace!

(It might be well to point out that the man who feels worthy of God is of all men most in need. This is self-righteousness!)

As the sick man is a candidate for the physician, so the sinful man is a candidate for the help of Jesus Christ.

"Come to me, all who labor and are heavy laden . . ."— Jesus Christ.

Preparedness

Twenty-nine men, women, and children boarded a crack Santa Fe train in Los Angeles Union Station one Sunday evening . . .

Fifteen minutes later they were in eternity!

They had boarded that train bound for San Diego or some intermediate point. Death was the farthest thing from their minds. Yet within a quarter of an hour it had struck!

Their minds and hearts were crowded with a multitude of emotions: memories of a happy weekend with friends, sadness at parting with loved ones for a short time (little did they know how long it would be), expectation of things awaiting them at their destination, loneliness . . .

They had plans—dreams—desires—ambitions. They expected these to be fulfilled. They were going to see to it that they were!

But in a matter of minutes the final curtain fell!

A few days later, a handsome, six-foot, keen-eyed eighteen-year-old high school boy dropped dead while rehearsing with his glee club.

Morbid to review this you say? No! Just realistic! We may not prevent tragedy, but at least we ought to learn from it. The learning process is often painful, but intelligent men do not discard it for that reason.

The point is not to frighten or alarm, but to stimulate a man to stop and think!

No man has a right to presume on life—to assume he's got so many years ahead. There is no security against this one inevitable appointment—death!

No man has a corner of life! At any moment, utterly unexpected, without the slightest warning it may come. Today might be *anyman's* last day on earth! Some man reading this selection could be gone fifteen minutes after he lays it down!

What quirk gets into a man's thinking that he will disregard this one great emergency? What makes an otherwise intelligent, farsighted business man ignore his "rendezvous with death"?

If there were no provision he could make—no way he could guarantee his eternal welfare—it would be understandable.

But the fact that God has made available in His Son a simple, sure, safe provision for eternal life, makes a man's neglect inexcusable!

Not that one should be preoccupied with death. That's just the point! Let a man put his trust in Christ's provision for forgiveness and eternal life . . . let him square himself with God on the basis of the cross . . . let him put himself in God's hands—line up with God's will . . . he can forget the "grim reaper." All is well for God's promise is unfailing.

"God so loved the world that he gave his only Son, that

whosoever believes in him should not perish but have eternal life" (John 3:16).

God in Focus

"I want a God with a face on," said a little girl to her minister one day.

Thereby expressing a child-like, nevertheless profound, desire for reality in religion. She was not satisfied with some nebulous, ethereal abstraction for God.

She wanted something definite, something tangible. She wanted a *someone* for a God . . . not a *something*.

Perhaps that is why men do not take God more seriously. They hold a theory about God: their notion of God is foggy, hazy, remote . . . an idea that is beyond them with no connection with the everyday.

A man wants a God with a face on!

"Who is the God you worship?" I have asked men this question on many occasions. "Tell me about Him. What is He like? Where does He dwell? Is He real to you?"

Again and again they stop after a few confused mutterings and admit God is quite unreal. When pinned down they have little to say. Why should a man bother about God if that is all He means to him?

But consider Jesus Christ!

Jesus Christ is *God in focus!* In Him we see God clearly—distinctly—sharply—down-to-earth!

In Jesus Christ God has made the fullest, broadest, highest revelation of Himself:

In many and various ways "God spoke of old to our fathers

24

by the prophets; but in these last days he has spoken to us by a Son!" (Heb. 1:1).

If you want to know what God is like, look at His Son. If you want to hear God, listen to His Son! *A man will make no mistake following Christ!*

Let a man begin with Jesus wherever he must to be honest with himself; let him investigate Jesus all the way. Let him go along with Jesus as far as truth dictates, as far as honest inquiry leads.

He will begin to realize that Jesus is God in focus!

He may begin his thinking with Jesus and God at opposite poles. But as he continues his investigation, he will discover that Jesus and God converge until they merge into one.

You can't go wrong trusting Christ—following Christ—worshiping Christ! He will lead you to a personal, dynamic experience of God.

"That which was from the beginning, which we have heard, which we have seen with our eyes, which we have looked upon and touched with our hands . . . we proclaim also to you, so that you may have fellowship with us; and our fellowship is with the Father and with his Son Jesus Christ" (1 John 1:1–3).

Man's First Duty

What is it that God wants from a man first of all? What is the first duty God requires? What is man's first obligation to his Creator? Get this settled—the door is open to maximum personal freedom and efficiency!

It is not a man's talent! Though it is a splendid thing when

25

a man surrenders great talent to God's service. Many Christian servants could have enjoyed tremendous success in business or industry or the professions or government. They dedicated that ability to God—used it for His glory. Yet God does not ask first for a man's talent . . . wonderful as that is!

Nor does God require a man's money! This also is certainly important! God's program on earth depends on the gifts of God's people. It is geared to the financial status quo. One thing that hinders the kingdom of God enterprise is lack of funds. Missionaries are sent—buildings are built—work is done—or left undone often—in ratio to the giving of Christian people.

It is highly debatable how much a man loves God, how sincere he is in his Christian profession, if he does not surrender his money to God. Yet money is not the thing God requires!

Neither is it a man's time God wants first! Though it's important! The work of the kingdom of God depends in large measure on the time that consecrated laymen give to it. The church program would suffer immeasurably if godly laymen did not give much of their time to the guidance of its business affairs. Yet important as a man's time is, it does not come first!

All these are important! All are part of the truth! No man takes God seriously who withholds his talent—his money—his time from God! The measure of a man's sincerity is the measure of his consecration of these things to Christ and His kingdom!

But there is something else, something absolutely basic, something without which nothing else a man gives means anything to God! Give God everything—without this, you've given Him nothing!

The first thing God wants from every man is the man himself! God wants you! Until He has you, He wants nothing from you. No gift is a substitute for yourself to God!

It is possible to own that which you do not possess! I own books that someone else possesses. They were borrowed. God owns the Christian man, purchased him by the blood of the cross of His Son . . . but God wants to possess that which He owns. He wants man to surrender himself willingly!

"I appeal to you therefore, brethren, by the mercies of God, to present your bodies as a living sacrifice, holy and acceptable to God, *which is your [reasonable service]* . . . " (Rom. 12:1).

Evaluation

This selection begins with a provocative and rather impertinent question—but think it through seriously. There's meat in it!

Suppose everyone else were just like you—what kind of a world would this be? What if everyone did as you do—emulated the example you give them—what would come of us?

What would happen to marriage, the home, the coming generation, if every husband were like you—treated his wife the way you treat yours . . . if every father were your kind of a father?

Suppose everyone else in your community took the same interest—felt the same responsibility—bore the same burden you do for civic and community affairs . . . what would become of your city?

Or if every citizen felt your allegiance—held the same concern for government—investigated election issues—went to the polls with the same regularity—voted with the same intelligence—kept in touch with the legislators as you . . . what would happen to the democratic process?

What if everyone were as humble as you—as selfless as you—as kind as you—as patient as you—as thoughtful as you? If all your friends were like yourself—would you enjoy being around them? Would you cultivate them? Would you want them as friends?

What if all men were your kind of a Christian—with your kind of dedication—your commitment—your devotion? What would happen to the church if all men supported it as you do? If all men honored the Lord in their homes—their jobs—their social lives the way you do . . . what would happen to His reputation?

Suppose everyone had the same burden for lost men you have—the same concern for those outside of Christ—showed the same interest in helping men to know God?

What if your son grows up to be just like you? He may! You owe it to him to be the kind of man whose example is safe to follow!

You see we all tend to "pass the buck"—to "let George do it." We cling tenaciously to our own little interests—never get excited until something begins to hurt us personally. With the result that evil forces operate almost unmolested to bring their devastation and ruin to America.

But we have no right to expect our liberties to be defended by other men, especially if we ourselves are not willing to pay the price of defense! The future of our world is a personal matter . . . it depends on each of us! Multiply your attitude—your outlook—your conduct by a few million to get an accurate picture of what our world is like!

"Walk worthy of the calling to which you have been called . . . " (Eph. 4:1).

Man's Touch

Have you ever stopped to think that it is the touch of human nature that spells the difference between right and wrong—good and evil?

It is not that things are good or bad in and of themselves, but it is the way man uses them that makes the difference!

Most things in this life are either a blessing or a curse, depending on what man does with them. This is the key to the solution of every problem!

Take for example the technological progress man has made in the past twenty years. Never in history has man's "know-how" been so finely developed. Yet man uses his gadgets and gimmicks selfishly—destructively . . . and turns a blessing into a curse.

The same is true with science. Its research and production have made immeasurable advances. Yet today the fruit of science is what man most fears. Not because it is in itself bad, but because of the possibilities of man's use of it!

Money is a blessing or a curse, depending on how man uses it. As long as man possesses his money—uses it wisely—it's a blessing to his life. But the minute money begins to possess the man—dictate to him—it is devastating.

Pleasure is a blessing or a curse. Some men live for pleasure—let it run . . . and ruin . . . their lives. Other men take pleasure as it comes, as a by-product of life, as one of the incidental returns of a life well lived. Then pleasure is constructive—edifying—productive . . . a blessing!

Even virtue can be a blessing or a curse! Let a man boast of his virtue—pride himself on his achievement morally—and he is drawn inevitably into self-righteous pharisaism. Virtue then becomes a vice.

Humility is a virtue. Let a man be self-conscious of his humility and he turns it into pride. Let him talk about his humility and he turns it into arrogance. Humility talked about is humility degenerated into conceit!

Jesus Christ Himself is a blessing or a curse, depending on what a man does with Him! He is either a man's *Savior* or a man's *Judge*. He either commends a man to God—or if a man refuses Christ—rejects Him; the man stands condemned by his rejection!

This is perfectly illustrated by the two thieves who hung on either side of Christ at His crucifixion. One appealed to Christ—asked for mercy. It was granted. The other rebelled—rejected. And he went out under his own condemnation. He was condemned by refusing the love that would redeem him!

"He who believes in him is not condemned; he who does not believe is condemned already, because he has not believed in the name of the only Son of God" (John 3:18).

Temptation

One thing that beats good Christian men is temptation. But the reason is simply because they do not understand the function of temptation in the life of the Christian.

Temptation has a place—a very important and vital role—in the growth of the man of God. Get this . . . *you can make every temptation contribute to your spiritual maturity.*

The first thing we need to know is that temptation in and of itself is not sin! Our Lord was tempted—"yet without sin." Not until a man yields to temptation does it become sin! Temptation is designed for spiritual exercise. Exercise helps a man grow strong—virile—efficient.

Many good and honorable men are plagued by thoughts that sometimes cross their minds: vile, selfish, lustful, unexplainable thoughts that pop up unexpectedly at the most surprising times. These thoughts are not sin! They do not become so unless a man entertains them—plays with them—encourages them—feeds them with imagination!

Or they are confused by mixed motives. A man can go along motivated by the highest purpose. Suddenly selfish goals cut across his consciousness; they take over and almost discourage him, make him feel like quitting.

When these thoughts—these false motives crowd in—a man has to remember that the choice is still with him! He is free to choose which thoughts he will let occupy his mind. He is still free to choose which motives he will follow!

It's how the man chooses—not the vile thoughts—not the selfish motives—that makes the sin. As long as a man lives he can expect to be confronted—at the most unexpected times—by fleshly suggestions. He does not have to yield to them!

Another thing to realize is that with every temptation God makes a way of escape. Man does not fight off temptation with his own thoughts or his own ideas—he fights temptation with the Word of God hidden in his heart. He does not resist temptation in his own strength.

The next thing to remember is that when a man does yield to temptation he should not give up! No matter how many times he falls on his face, he is not licked unless he stays there. God the Father is always ready to forgive and cleanse. His grace is sufficient!

A father teaches his infant son to walk. When the child falls, the father does not leave him there and give it up as a bad job. On the contrary, he picks up the child and patiently encourages his halting steps again and again until he walks on his own.

Our heavenly Father is no less a Father than this. He does not want us to fall, but He does not give us up for lost when we do. In His love He sent His Son to die as a covering for sin. In that sacrifice every man who wants it has forgiveness as often as he needs it. The only requirement is honest confession—honest turning to the Lord.

"If we confess our sins, he is faithful and just, and will forgive our sins, and cleanse us from all unrighteousness" (1 John 1:9).

Human Goodness Deceptive

In one way, a "good man" is the strongest argument against Jesus Christ and His crucifixion!

If a man can be good enough—godly enough—by his own efforts and in his own strength—it was unnecessary for Christ to die on a cross! At least for some men.

And if the death of Christ was unnecessary, His coming to earth was unnecessary. Because He came as "The Lamb of God that taketh away the sin of the world." Not just an example—not just a teacher—but a sacrifice for sin!

He did not come primarily to lay down an ethical system that man must struggle to keep. He came to provide a power whereby a man could overcome the sin in his life. He came to die for man's sin, to rise again for man's justification. He came to redeem!

But Christ will not—cannot—help the man who refuses to admit his need. The man who thinks he is "good enough" in himself is outside the circle of Christ's redemptive power.

This was precisely why He was so grossly misunderstood by the Pharisees. Being members of the strictest religious group of their day, and being regimented from dawn to dusk by a rigid system of laws and duties, they felt they were good enough. Actually they were not interested in what God required . . . only in their own achievement.

In fact they prided themselves on this. And their self-righteousness built up a wall about them even Jesus Christ could not penetrate. *Self-righteousness equals righteousness by self!*

The Pharisees were the conventional, self-respecting "good men" of Jesus' day. For them He could do nothing! Because they would not admit their need.

When they asked Him why He continually fraternized with disreputable people, He replied, "Those who are well have no need of a physician, but those who are sick; I have not come to call the righteous, but sinners to repentance" (Luke 5:31–32).

But these "good men" missed the point of that razorsharp sarcasm. They were so insulated by their own righteousness that the piercing truth of His words could not get through. Religious innoculation made them immune to truth!

The plain fact is that God has declared all men to be sinners. No exceptions! That includes you and me. It includes most of all the "good man"—the professionally religious man—who refuses to see his own need of God's grace!

"Since all have sinned and fall short of the glory of God, they are justified by his grace as a gift, redemption which is in Christ Jesus . . . " (Rom. 3:23).

Guilt and Its Remedy

Nothing can mess up a man's life or increase complications like the irreparable past!

It can be a steady and persistent drain on a man's energy—rob him of his efficiency—clog his mental and spiritual machinery—cut down his drive to sub-zero.

What does a man do with his mistakes, the failures, the defeats, the sin of the past? Like a hideous infection they pollute all his ambitions and dreams and determination for the future!

Just about the time a man figures he's on his way, he's reminded of some unspeakable thing in his past that shames him utterly. Like a thick smog it blots out the sunshine of hope for the future. Memory of failure and defeat suck at his vitality; they leave him weak and whipped.

A fellow sometimes gets to the place where he feels "What's the use?" Dogged with failure, defeat, and sin he's tempted to give up. Like an octopus the tentacles of guilt grip him—squeeze the vision out of him.

Where's the answer to this experience so normal to the average man? What's the solution to this awful plague of the irretrievable past with its burning shame—its silent mockery of a man's effort for the future?

Lady Macbeth tried to remove the guilt by washing. "Out—out damned spot!" she cried. But the spot remained!

Pilate called for a basin of water and tried the same thing. "I'll have nothing to do with this just person . . . " he stated. But the deed was done. He felt the weight of the guilt. He could not escape.

Judas went back to the chief priests and begged them to take back the thirty pieces of silver—the price of his shameful betrayal. They would not taint their fingers with the plagued coins. Judas cast the silver on the floor of the temple and went out and hanged himself.

What price will a man pay to forget? To have blotted from

his memory the deeds of the past? No price is too great! But is there a remedy?

There is a remedy! And wonder of wonders, it is free! That doesn't mean it's cheap; it's the most costly purchase ever made in history. Jesus Christ paid it! So it's free to us. Here again is the reason Christian faith is valid. It has the answer!

It has a power that can blot out the past—remove it—cleanse it . . . as though it had never happened. This is not something to be debated. This is something to be tried. "The blood of Jesus his Son cleanses us from all sin. . . ." It works! It clears a man!

"I am not ashamed of the gospel; it is the power of God for salvation to every one who has faith . . ." (Rom. 1:16).

Self-management

No man can do his best tied in knots! Tension in the life is like friction in machinery. It slows a man down. If allowed to continue it can "freeze" him into inaction.

And the great shame is that normally the things that tie a man in knots are things over which he has no control.

No man gets tied up over something he knows he can handle. It's the thing beyond his reach or control that does it. Things that seem for the moment too big for him—uncertainties. The past and the future are both beyond his reach. They should not be allowed to clutter up the present!

Therefore the problem of pressure resolves to this question: What does a man do with the things he can't handle . . . things beyond his reach?

Some men, filled with false pride, refuse to admit there is

anything they can't handle. Which only increases the tension! Because not only do they have the problem itself to worry about . . .

They add to the confusion—deceive themselves—put themselves on the spot. Then it's not just a matter of handling a thing for the sake of getting it done, but of handling it to avoid humiliation.

Not just the problem now, but pride that grips the man—dictates his action—rules it over him—increases the tension! It winds him up tight!

Such artificial pride really puts a fellow behind the eight ball! The intelligent man plays it smart—stays out of such a stupid hole.

The wise man knows how to delegate—how to turn a thing over to a specialist—and relax in the confidence the specialist knows what he's doing. That's management! Meanwhile he goes about his business relaxed—efficient—productive!

It's smart to be a Christian, to walk the Christian way! The smart Christian man takes God into his confidence. The Bible makes it clear that God is interested in the details of a man's life. God wants to lift burdens—wants to help a man—wants to make the man a credit as a Christian.

The smart humble man knows how to turn things over to the Lord and let Him handle them! He knows nothing is too hard for God. "With God all things are possible." Trusting God he goes about his business free—easy—sharp—cool!

There is nothing mysterious about this. Like committing anything to a specialist, turning things over to God is a matter of decision. Having decided, the man asks God's help in prayer—lets God take over in his life—trusts Him!

"Commit your way to the Lord; trust in him, and he will act" (Ps. 37:5).

God Cares

It's always too soon to quit! Always too soon to give up! Always to soon to surrender to self-despair!

An incident reported once in the Los Angeles papers emphasizes this. The incident: A young man jumped to his death from the window of a large downtown hotel.

Behind that suicide lay an amazing and pathetic story. The young man had run up a batch of bills—including his hotel bill—with no money to pay them. In his concern he wired a brother for help. But the money did not come.

Driven to distraction by the pressure, the young man took what seemed to him the only way out. It was the way of despair.

But the real tragedy was this: at the very moment he took his suicidal leap there was a letter waiting for him at the lobby desk . . . a letter with more than enough money to cover his bills. *If he'd only waited.*

The tragedy was so deep—so poignant—because it was so unnecessary! But that is the way of self-despair.

It's always too soon to quit! No matter how dark things look. No matter how insoluble the problem—how impossible—how imponderable—despair is never justified.

Because to despair of self is really to despair of God! It is to count God incapable—to measure God by human standards—to ignore the clear Word of God.

Nothing is too hard for God! With Him all things are possible! This is a truth men have tested and tried again and again to their satisfaction. Not once has God failed to help the man who called on Him for help. Not once have His promises been found wanting.

Self-despair is a scandal against God, because God has explicitly declared His interest and concern and love for *every man.* Jesus Christ insisted that the heavenly Father yearns to help those who need Him. All they need to do is *ask!*

The God who flung the stars into space, who knows when a sparrow falls to the ground, who has clothed the lilies of the field with greater glory than Solomon's . . . this same God is interested in each of us!

Whether the burden is domestic, business, financial, or personal, the heavenly Father desires to help those who come to Him with their need. Only false pride would keep a man from coming.

He cares for you! Cast your burden on the Lord.

Faithfulness

One of the rare qualities of leadership is faithfulness. That doesn't sound like much on the surface, but it's absolutely basic to worthwhileness.

The fellow who can stick to a thing—see it through—fight to the finish—is the man who adds up accomplishment in life.

Remember the story of the hare and tortoise? The hare had speed—show—glamour . . . played to the crowds—had them all on his side . . . but the tortoise won!

It takes more grace to go the daily round, to be faithful in small duties, to see things through . . . than it does to go through the crises of life.

Somehow nature compensates in crisis. Many people go

through storms without leaning too heavily on God. But it takes plenty of God's grace to stick at a thing day after day with dogged perseverance!

It's comparatively easy to be heroic when the crowd's watching—cheering. But it takes a good man to keep at it when nobody's paying attention!

Think of men who were faithful—who stayed with a thing—long after others had quit. Stuck it out through bitter criticism—ridicule . . . in spite of scorn and cynicism . . . in spite of failure—weariness—heartbreak. With rugged, stubborn faithfulness, they produced.

Men like Thomas Edison, Louis Pasteur, Pierre Curie, Henry Ford, and scores of others who sweat out hundreds of mistakes—failures—contempt—loneliness . . . and won unheard of victories—invaluable triumphs!

Contrast the men who started something in a flash of glamour but didn't hold on. Men who let go when the going was tough. Who took failure as final. Quit. Sometimes inches from their goal!

The thing that makes an English bulldog such a terrible foe is his ability to hang on. Once he gets hold of a thing he simply refuses to let go. He whips dogs twice—ten times—his size because he hangs on!

The world is crowded with little men who do nothing without recognition, who can't stand one failure, who fear mistakes, and who won't do one thing more than they're paid to do. Men who start clearing the desk at five to five. They stay little . . . won't be missed when they're gone!

There are never enough faithful men. Big men who can take criticism or ridicule or failure. Who stick at it through every conceivable pressure, until the job's done! Men who do a thing because it needs doing, for the sake of getting it done, not for the credit—whether they're seen or not. Men who never watch the clock!

"It is required of stewards that they be found trustworthy" (1 Cor. 4:2).

Perfect Timing

God's timing is never off! Never too slow—never too fast . . . always right on the nose! When God runs a man's life the schedule is a perfect one.

This is important to realize because there are times in a man's life when he wonders if maybe God has forsaken him. He feels that the Lord has left him to his own way and lets himself in for worry and discouragement that are unnecessary.

Just as a good steel man knows the proper temperatures, changes, length of time to produce the kind of metal he wants, so God knows exactly what pressures—what temperatures—will produce the right kind of a man.

Should God heed our wishes in the matter, we'd probably come off second best. We wouldn't grow into the kind of man God wants . . . the kind of a man we really want to be.

The man who has learned to trust God never questions when things do not work out the way he thinks they should. Chances are that which will get the man most is this business of timing.

He'll be inclined to feel that the heat's been on long enough. He'll be inclined to move up the schedule somewhat. But the wise man waits it out, knowing God's wisdom is perfect in the matter. God never makes a mistake!

To change the analogy a trifle: God knows when a man's cooked long enough. He knows the proper mixture of things to put into a man's life—the proper time to put him in the oven—the correct temperature . . . and the proper time to take him out.

God does not specialize in half-baked goods. He turns out a man just right always.

When trouble strikes a man, this is the secret of turning tragedy into triumph: take the trouble as an instrument in God's hand to make you the man you ought to be. Not that God is responsible for the trouble . . . but He will use it to your benefit.

Naturally this pressure, this heat, is not a pleasant experience. But it works good in the life of the man who will turn to the Lord in the midst of trials, who will yield to the Lord's will in the matter.

No man is ever whipped who turns to God in the midst of reverses. This is the secret of victory in life—victory over all things that may ruin another man.

"For the moment all discipline seems painful rather than pleasant; later it yields the peaceful fruit of righteousness to those who have been trained by it" (Heb. 12:11).

Perfect Love

Why does God love us?

Have you ever stopped to think about this? Have you ever asked yourself this question, "Why should God love me?" What is there about us that would make us beloved of God?

If a man really took this seriously and examined his own life in the light of God's truth he'd likely come up with the query, "What is man that thou art mindful of him?" Facing himself honestly, he'd probably ask, "Why should God bother about me?"

The fact is that God loves us because *God is love!*

There's a world of difference between the love of God and the love of man. As a matter of fact, in the original language of the New Testament, the Greek has a different word for God's love.

Man's love is a fragile thing: vacillating, uncertain, intermittent, transient. It is inclined to be selfish and demanding and possessive.

Man's love depends on the one he loves. A man loves one who is attractive—desirable—lovable. He does not love the one who is unlovely—unattractive—undesirable. He is repulsed by unlovable people.

Consequently a man cannot count on the love of his fellow man unless he earns that love. If he is not lovable he will probably not be loved. If there is not something within him that stimulates the love of another, he is starved for love.

The love of God is completely different!

God's love is utterly dependable—constant—certain.

Because the love of God depends not on the one who is being loved but on the One who is loving. God's love does not depend on the beloved—but on the lover.

God loves a man—not because the man is attractive or lovable—but because it is God's nature to love. God loves because He is love!

For God not to love would be for God to violate His own nature. Therefore the most unattractive man who ever lived is a candidate for God's love. God is true to His nature.

God loves us whether we deserve to be loved or not.

Whether there is anything within us to merit His love or not, we can count on Him to love us.

Of course if a man rejects God's love there is nothing God can do about it. For God to force a man would be contrary to the way of love. Love is not force. God loves a man enough to let him be free to reject that love.

"God shows his love for us in that while we were yet sinners Christ died for us" (Rom. 5:8).

Strategy of Waiting

Some men just have the knack for getting rich!

This idea came out in conversation with a friend whose position brings him into contact with many wealthy men. Someone had suggested to him that the ability to make money is a gift—like musical talent for example. Men are born with it.

Of course there are those who acquire it, who learn how to handle money wisely . . . but many are born with the aptitude. Everything they touch turns to gold. They seem to have a "nose" for it . . . a kind of "sixth sense" about investment and finance.

This friend said he had observed carefully in recent years a number of men who have this knack for making a million dollars. He noticed that one thing was characteristic of every one of them. Without one exception they had *patience!* They knew how to wait!

One man bought stock at $15. He didn't get hysterical when it dropped. He sweated it out . . . waited until the stock rose to $60. It took years . . . but he waited!

Another man purchased a parcel of ground for $50,000. Then he "sat on it" for years. And finally sold it for $500,000. He made hundreds of thousands of dollars . . . just waiting! Said my friend, "I wouldn't do that. The minute the stock began to slide I'd get scared. If it dropped too far, I'd get hysterical and sell out. If I owned the property, one scare would be enough to make me unload. Or if there were much pressure to sell out at a mild profit, I would yield."

Waiting—the wisest strategy of life.

Men who know how to wait are always at a premium. Not just in money matters . . . but in everything! Trouble is that a man goes through a trial—some testing period—and he acts as though God is dead—or disinterested. Forgetting God under pressure, he cracks.

But you say there's a difference: The reason the wealthy man can wait is because he has resources while he waits. Precisely! And the point of waiting on God is that God Himself is the resource of the man who has learned to wait on Him!

God has promised that "*all things* work together for good to them that love him. . . ." But we act as though God has not spoken. Or if He has, His word cannot be trusted. We act as though God is indifferent—or out of touch.

Instead of waiting on Him, we get fussed and confused—precipitate a foolish situation that adds to the confusion. In the name of common sense we yield to hysteria or self-despair. We run off in all directions to solve the dilemma . . . and end up strapped and worn out. Our efforts have only made matters worse. Our so-called common sense has been futile!

The man who waits on God *never* waits too long! He finds things work out right . . . and he's a better man for waiting!

"They who wait for the Lord shall renew their strength . . . " (Isa. 40:31).

The Truly Independent Man

"God helps those who help themselves."
For years I believed this was a quotation from the Bible! I heard it so often—and it sounded so pious. I was amazed to learn it was not Scripture.

Not only is it not in the Bible . . . it is utterly contrary to it.

It sounds practical and reasonable and strong on the surface. But actually it is just another subtle expression of man's pride. It is this kind of logic that makes it easy for a man to remain independent of God—and at the same time justify his independence with pious platitudes.

The fact is, it is man's pride in his own strength—his own adequacy—that prohibits him from turning to God in admission of need. "Bloody but unbowed," man's ego cries out, "I am the master of my fate. I am the captain of my soul!" Such godless thinking breeds the swastika and the hammer and sickle.

False pride eggs a man on, forces him to fight his own battles—make his own way—carry his own freight. This way a man can give himself the credit. This is the subtle sin in the process: Beholden to no one . . . not even God!

Out of this false view of strength comes such declarations as: "Religion is an opiate." The implication being that Christianity turns a man into a parasite—a jelly fish without drive or initiative or dependability.

Independence is the by-word of this false view . . . and it holds that the only dependable man is the one who is independent.

The outcome though, is independence from God. And independence from God leads inevitably to hopeless dependence. Just look anywhere behind the iron curtain. There dwell the least independent people in the world . . . the slaves of a system that cried, "Religion is an opiate." Declare your independence from God!

"Governed by God . . . or ruled by tyrants!" This is the real option in life. There is no third alternative . . . no neutrality!

This page had its birth when a friend was called upon to preach in his church on Laymen's Sunday. He asked himself what true independence meant. Came up with this idea: Real independence comes when a man lives in dependence on God!

Of course! A man's greatest drive and initiative and efficiency and productivity come when he declares his dependence on God! Until then he is something less than the man he could be. "The man who kneels before God can stand up to anything." The man is most dependable who depends on God!

"And [the Lord] said to me, 'My grace is sufficient for you, for my power is made perfect in weakness' . . . when I am weak, then I am strong" (2 Cor. 12:9, 10).

True Righteousness and Its Counterfeit

True righteousness is effortless! It does not come by struggle. If a man is striving to be good—he is failing. This is inevitable.

The Bible recognizes two kinds of righteousness: human

and divine. That which is man-made—and that which is God-given.

One is the product of man's effort . . . the other is the gift of God!

When men struggle to be righteous, they end up in one of two places: either in the pride of their achievement, or in the despair of failure.

And both pride and despair are wrong: because pride says God is unnecessary . . . and despair says God is unable.

Thus human righteousness not only does not please God . . . it turns out to be an abomination to Him. In the final analysis it is man coming to God on his own conditions. Which is impertinence to say the least!

Actually the most subtle, the most insidious opposition to God is expressed in human goodness that is utterly independent of God. This kind of righteousness put the Son of God on the cross. It was this same spirit that stoned and killed the prophets of Israel in Old Testament days.

True righteousness begins when a man admits his sin and need—turns to God in humility for forgiveness and strength.

As a man yields to the love of God—commits his way to God daily—God goes to work in that man's life giving him the strength—the joy—the beauty—the health of holiness . . . genuine holiness . . . not piety.

True righteousness is what the Bible calls "the fruit of the Spirit." And it grows in the man as effortlessly as fruit grows on the tree.

This righteousness breeds attractive, strong humility in a man because he is always aware of his dependence on God. As he is dependent on the atmosphere for breath, he is dependent on God for spiritual health.

Human righteousness tries to be humble. But it sticks out

like a sore thumb. Man-made humility is obnoxious. Actually it is pride turned inside out. (Humility and how I attained it.) There is nothing you can do with a conceited man when the very essence of his conceit is that he thinks he is humble.

Man-made righteousness becomes censorious and hard and critical. It is always looking down its nose at others . . . always indicting and condemning.

It makes issues of petty things: it "strains at a gnat and swallows a camel." It criticizes the speck in another's eye, and disregards the log in his own.

"I bear them witness that they have a zeal for God, but it is not enlightened. For, being ignorant of the righteousness that comes from God, and seeking to establish their own, they did not submit to God's righteousness" (Rom. 10:2, 3).

Fabulous Proposition

What a fabulous proposition God offers man!

Three great truths underlie the Bible theme. Three things that help a man appreciate the down-to-earthness—the sheer workableness of the gospel.

First: God loves man and He is aggressive in this love! God has taken the initiative toward man . . . in spite of man's failure to love God. We do not love God. If a man is honest, he must admit this!

The average man gives very little, if any, attention to God. Once in a while we think about God, but not for very long— nor with much intensity. It is quite obvious that the Bible is correct when it says, "No man seeks after God." God seeking—God concern is not exactly characteristic of us as a nation or as individuals.

Furthermore, our attitude toward God could hardly be called love. In spite of the fact that the first and great commandment demands it! And if the greatest commandment is to love God, the greatest sin is not to love God!

To be perfectly frank and honest, the average of us doesn't bother much about God. This is the fundamental point of the Bible theme!

But even though man does not take God seriously—even though man is a sinner—the Bible declares that God loves him. God loves the sinner! God loves the worst sinner who ever lived. He hates his sin, but He loves him! As the physician works to heal the sick, God works to save the sinner.

God took the initiative. He loved man so much He sent His only Son into the world to redeem man. Even when a man runs from God, God goes after him. He is a seeking, loving, persevering God.

Second: God meets man on the basis of divine grace! Not on the basis of man's worthiness. Not on the basis of a man's merit. But on the grounds of God's mercy and grace. Grace means unmerited favor!

We deserve a penalty. We get love! As a matter of fact, the one thing that qualifies a man for God's help is need—sin. The greater a man's sin, the more he qualifies for grace. It is man's need, not his goodness, that makes him eligible for God. (Just as it is his illness, not his health, that qualifies him for the physician.)

Third: the only thing that prevents a man from receiving God's love is the man himself. If a man will not recognize his need—will not acknowledge his sin—he is not a candidate for

God's grace, any more than he would be a candidate for medical aid if he refused to admit sickness.

God loves him—God wants to help. God will supply all the healing grace that is needed. The greater the sin—the more grace is available. But if the man refuses to receive it, God will not force His love on that man!

It's not the sinner God can't help. It's the man who thinks he's righteous! "God so loved the world that He gave . . . " (John 3:16). "Where sin increased, grace abounded all the more . . . " (Rom. 5:20).

The Man God Uses

A man is often inclined to assume that God cannot use him because he has no special talent or ability. He's apt to feel God uses only the specialist with unique and powerful aptitudes.

But the run-of-the-mill man (with just ordinary qualifications) doesn't have a place in God's program because he has nothing to offer God . . . nothing for God to work with so to speak.

Which is to miss the truth by a mile! God is not a respecter of persons. He is not partial. God uses committed men—talented or not!

Actually the only ability God requires is *availability!* When God finds a man willing to be used, there is no limit to what He can do through that man!

Someone has put it this way: "God can do a lot with a little, providing He has all there is of it!"

Because the resources are God's, not man's! God does not depend on human resources. He is the Creator God who can make something out of nothing! God can begin with nothing . . . and produce!

But God's method is men. God works through men! Through the committed man He pours His inexhaustible resources to meet the world's need.

In fact, it is precisely here that many a man with special ability fails: He counts on his ability instead of God. Feeling he has a great deal on the ball, he is inclined to work in his own strength—depend on his own talent.

And his ability—instead of being a help to God—gets in the way and hinders the work God wants to do in the man.

Of course, such a man can accomplish a great deal, but in the final analysis his work is limited because at best his resources are limited. He may seem to succeed, but he is able to do only what he is able to do!

Whereas the man who has learned to trust in God rather than his own ability does infinitely more than he himself is able to do, for God works through the man using His unlimited resources.

This is not to say that God does not use the talented man, but it is to insist that God can do infinitely more with the humble and committed man than He can do with a man who trusts himself only—no matter how talented he may seem to be!

God uses consecrated talent. But He uses the man who is available—able or not—rather than the man who is able but uncommitted.

"I appeal to you therefore, brethren, by the mercies of God, to present your bodies as a living sacrifice, acceptable to God, which is your [reasonable service] . . ." (Rom. 12:1).

51

Kingdom Enterprise

Stewardship begins with the fact that life is a trust from God! Everything a man has—everything he is—comes from Him. God is "the giver of every good and perfect gift."

A man comes into the world with nothing . . . he leaves with nothing. Naked he enters—naked he leaves! What he does with what's here between his entrance and exit comes under the heading of stewardship.

The mighty vast resources of God are waiting for a man when he arrives. All the raw materials to build a life (for time and eternity) are here for him. He has the option of using them—or abusing them. He can exploit these golden opportunities—or neglect them. The point is, *it's up to him!*

The wise steward—seeing life as a trust from God—determines to buy up every opportunity to be productive, to glorify God by his use of the raw materials. He does not bury his talent for fear of losing it . . . he invests it in the hope of returns: thirty-fold—sixty-fold—hundred-fold!

The foolish man either neglects his opportunities and just vegetates . . . or he abuses the opportunities by prostituting them on useless programs and plans. He's either a clod—or a clown!

Obviously the wisest investment is that which takes into consideration the primary interests of the Lord.

It is perfectly clear in the gospels that the primary interest of Jesus Christ was the glory of God through the salvation of men. He came into the world to "seek and save the lost." His mission was to die on the cross for the redemption of the world.

And the last thing He gave to His church was this mandate:

To preach the gospel to all the world and every creature . . . making disciples of all nations! This world mission
of the church is the nearest thing to the heart of Jesus Christ!

That church that fails to put this world mission first repudi-
ates its right to be identified with Christ. That Christian who
neglects this mandate that Christ laid to the charge of every
disciple is something less than a Christian!

Of course the Christian man who takes the long look—who
has vision—sees this world enterprise of Jesus Christ to be the
soundest investment he can make. It pays off in eternity . . .
and it pays off right now!

Nothing is wasted that is dedicated to the kingdom of
Christ and His work in the world. Every investment of time
and energy and talent and money realizes dividends—everlasting dividends . . . plus the deepest, broadest, highest, soundest satisfactions in this life!

This is irresistible logic: That a man is most a man when he
gives himself to God and lines up with God's program . . .
that he enters into his true destiny when he invests everything
he can in the fulfillment of God's eternal purpose!

"He who finds his life will lose it, and he who loses his life
for my sake will find it" (Matt. 10:39).

Short Cuts

Someone has described sin as a short cut. Stealing is a short
cut to work. Lust is a short cut to love. Adultery is a short cut
to marriage. Idolatry is a short cut to faith.

Hardly a day goes by but that the Christian man is tempted

to take some short cut in his life or business. And at first glance it looks like the short cut would pay off.

It may pay off—with some quick and transient satisfaction—but in the long run it turns to ashes! After the short-term pay-off comes the kickback! There's a reason for this—a very sound reason, if a man will take the time to think it through.

The wise man learns to count on certain factors that may not be apparent on the surface—factors that don't show up to the shallow thinker. He knows he can depend on them. He operates on the basis of them.

At first his decision may look foolish in the light of observable data, but he has mastered the art of taking into consideration certain other facts that are just as valid—even though invisible.

The greatest fact to count on is God! And the man who does is the man who ultimately wins! He's basing his operation on bed-rock reality!

God's way is the way of the right—the way of truth—the way of honesty. When a man does the right thing—even though it seems all the powers of hell are opposed—he can be sure God is on his side. Or to put it in Lincoln's words: He is on God's side! This is the vital factor.

Any man doing business in our modern world will be tempted to take certain short cuts. They look practical enough, and with a little rationalizing they can be made to seem right.

The trouble comes when a man leaves God out of consideration. He takes the short cut . . . and regrets it desperately afterward.

Even though there's nothing tremendous at stake he's been unfaithful to his conscience. He's violated his own integrity—and it's a bitter pill to swallow! He tries to salve his conscience—tries to justify the short cut—but it doesn't work. He's failed himself. And grieved God!

There's no percentage in this kind of a deal!

Had he taken God into his calculations he would have known the only intelligent course was God's way, a way that guarantees deep-down satisfaction immediately . . . and the right kind of dividends long term.

No man can fail when he's on God's side! It may look like he is along the way . . . but at the finish, the balance is clearly in the favor of the man who takes God seriously! And until the outcome is final, he's able to live with himself because the peace of God rules in his life!

"If God is for us, who is against us?" (Rom. 8:31).

Money—Blessing or Curse

Money—little or much—will lead to the greatest blessing in a man's life when used God's way. Used wrongly, it becomes the worst curse to a man!

Man was made to be a channel, not a reservoir! Serious complications are inevitable in a man's body when there is not a balance of intake and elimination. The same is true mentally: The more a man uses his mind the sharper it becomes, the greater load it is able to carry.

Use muscle and it gets strong and supple. Neglect muscle and it deteriorates. This is health in every realm: balance between income and outgo—intake and elimination. When life begins to store up for the sake of storing up, destructive processes are set in motion. Life begins to stagnate.

And money is the most subtly destructive thing a man

handles in a normal lifetime. It sneaks up on a man. Before he knows it, he's no longer making money—money is making him. He no longer possesses it—it possesses him! That's why the Bible speaks of "the deceitfulness of riches."

But only as a man insists on being a reservoir can this happen. As long as he handles money as a trust from God to be used wisely with God in mind . . . as long as he's a channel—lets money go through him—it leads to supreme blessing. It blesses those benefited by it . . . but most of all it blesses the giver!

Not that a man should be careless with money. On the contrary, a sense of accountability to God will make a man a careful steward—faithful in the disbursement and investment of the funds over which God has given him control.

Money is coined talent and energy and time. It is coined life! Money represents a man's effort and ingenuity and achievement. Dedicated to God it represents a man's best consecrated to the highest. The man who invests his money in God's kingdom is investing his life as surely as the preacher—the evangelist—the missionary.

The man who dedicates his money is dedicating himself. And it follows conversely that the man who refuses to dedicate his money to God has not really committed himself!

Just as God uses men to work His program in the world, so God uses money. Not that God is poor—or helpless—or man indispensable . . . simply that this is the way God has chosen to do. God's program is geared to the economy just as other things are. It moves or stalls in terms of money available just as other programs do. When God has a job to do, He not only looks for men to work . . . He looks for men to give!

It is impossible to outgive God. He will be no man's debtor. When God finds a man who will be a channel instead of a reservoir, He pours out blessing beyond measure on that man. And the greatest of all blessings is that such a man is part of God's program: The great cosmic—divine—eternal program!

"Give, and it will be given to you; good measure, pressed down, shaken together, running over . . . " (Luke 6:38).

Success in Business— Failure at Home

Have you ever thought how strange it is that there are men who succeed at everything else—and fail with their family? They know how to build a business, but fail miserably when it comes to building a home.

Some time ago an attractive woman came to the office for counseling. She was beside herself. She lived in a spacious ranch house in Southern California, with a kidney-shaped swimming pool in the back yard, and drove her own Cadillac convertible.

She and her husband had two lovely children. Outwardly it would seem they had everything a man and wife could want. But their marriage was falling apart. Their home was folding . . . and she was desperate.

Every time she tried to discuss the failure of the marriage with her husband he refused to acknowledge it. Didn't figure anything was wrong. He argued, "Don't I give you and the children everything? You have your own car, a lovely home, fashionable clothing—and the children don't lack a thing! Plenty of women would give anything to have what you have!" That's the way his mind worked. Discussion was futile with him.

He was giving his family everything . . . with one terrible exception: *he was not giving them himself!* They had all the creature comforts—luxuries galore—but they didn't have him or his love and affection.

He was harnessed to his work seven days a week, twelve to fourteen hours a day. When he did relax, which was exceedingly rare, it meant a few lines of bowling with the boys, a round of golf with a client, or some time at the club . . . stag! He was always too busy for his children.

He wasn't running around with other women. He never got drunk. He wasn't a playboy. He drove himself relentlessly. He was determined to let nothing stand in the way of his success.

But the tragedy was that he couldn't see he was making a nasty failure of the most important thing in his life. He was failing the very ones he was trying so hard to succeed for. He was failing his family as much as if he had deserted them!

Said his wife, "I'd give everything we have just to have my husband together with us."

This is marriage: for a husband and wife to possess each other. And if they don't—no matter what else they possess—their marriage is a flop!

This man was admired and respected by outsiders—emulated by subordinates in the business. No one doubted he would reach the top before he was fifty. He was a glowing success in business . . . and a pathetic failure in life!

The man that neglects his family—however he may succeed before the world—is a failure before God. Next to man's relationship with the Lord, his relationship to his wife and children is most important.

"Husbands, love your wives, as Christ loved the church and gave himself up for her. . . . Fathers, do not provoke your children to anger, but bring them up in the discipline and instruction of the Lord" (Eph. 5:25; 6:4).

Doubt or Unbelief

There is a radical difference between doubt and unbelief! One is a matter of the intellect. The other (though disguising itself as intellectual) is basically a matter of the will. Doubt is difficulty in understanding . . . unbelief is disobedience!

Follow the record of the life and ministry of Jesus Christ in the New Testament and you become aware of a strong divergence among His followers:

One group—though they find it difficult to understand and accept the things they see and hear—continue to follow Jesus with open hearts and minds. He is an enigma to them— nevertheless they continue to trust Him!

They cannot explain what they see and hear. Neither can they deny these things! They cannot logically account for Jesus Christ—yet in the integrity of their hearts they admit to the facts and continue to follow Him faithfully. They doubt . . . but they do not reject Him!

The other group (unbelievers) cannot deny the facts. They are indisputable. But they try to explain them away. They cannot account for Jesus Christ. And they refuse to give in— refuse to yield to Him!

They continue to follow Jesus—but for ulterior purposes. They are out to get Him! They ask questions—not because they seek an answer—but in the hope of discrediting Him. They try to catch Him off guard, hang Him on the thorns of a dilemma, set up situations that will allow them to bring an indictment and conviction so they can liquidate Him.

The heart of unbelief is rejection of anything that interferes with the self-life—anything that injures pride and vanity. Unbelief argues against truth because it does not want to commit itself to truth.

The doubter cannot explain the facts, but he admits them. The unbeliever refuses to acknowledge the facts, and uses intellectual reasons as an excuse! He tries to discredit the facts because he is not willing to obey the truth!

Unbelief is disobedience wearing a robe of false intellectualism or religiosity. Actually, unbelief is immoral. It is at bottom dishonest!

There is no logical reason for rejecting the truth as it is in Jesus Christ. The evidence is overwhelming. The New Testament contains a historical record that is absolutely trustworthy. In every generation there are millions of men and women who testify to the relevancy—the validity of the gospel. Jesus Christ works when men try Him!

But unbelief hardens its heart against the truth and refuses to yield! Like the sign on the desk of a military official in Tokyo headquarters: "Don't confuse me with the facts—I've already made up my mind!"

The apostle Peter says: "We did not follow cleverly devised myths when we made known to you the power and coming of our Lord Jesus Christ, but we were eyewitnesses of his majesty." Jesus said: "If any man will do God's will he shall know the truth. . ."

Trouble or Triumph?

I saw an insurance ad the other day. "Don't let the same accident hurt you twice!" That's sound wisdom for other areas of life also. Of course an accident can hurt twice: When it happens—and when you have to pay for it!

In the same way a man can let difficulty or failure or defeat do double duty in his life. Double trouble! When it happens—and after it happens *depending on how he takes it.*

You may not be able to prevent what happens to you . . . but you can decide what it is going to do to you after it happens! Whether it ruins or makes a man depends on what he lets it do to him!

The trouble that ruins one man—because he feels sorry for himself—makes another man—because he accepts the trouble as part of life—as an opportunity for growth and development.

The defeat or failure that breaks one man—because he takes it as final—builds another man—because he takes it as a lesson to be learned. He looks for a lesson in every difficulty. Lets trouble teach him!

(Edison had failed a thousand times in one experiment. His assistant was ready to give up in discouragement and admit failure. Not Edison! "This is no time to quit," he said, "we know a 1000 things that won't work." He turned every failure into final success!)

(Before Henry Ford was half-way through building his first car he knew it wouldn't work. Friends urged him to drop the whole ridiculous plan. But he refused. He finished the car—learned things he would never have known otherwise. Ford began with a job that was a failure half-way through. He ended up by leaving more than 100 million to posterity.)

Whether misfortune adds up to a stumbling block or a stepping stone depends entirely on how a man takes it—what he does with it after it happens! Troubles are inevitable in life. It's up to each man as to what he's going to do with them!

One man whines—babies himself—immerses himself in self-pity—feeds his ego on his own sympathy—lets himself be preoccupied with his dark circumstances. Nobody else ever had it so bad, he figures. Of course he's whipped! He not only has trouble. He nurses it along! Gets bitter—cynical!

Actually it's a matter of decision! A man decides whether he's going to feel sorry for himself and whine and mope around like an adolescent . . . or whether he's going to turn the tragedy into triumph—defeat into victory—failure into success. It's up to him how he takes it!

The best insurance against double trouble is the realization that God's grace is sufficient for every need. God will not spare a man trouble . . . but He will help a man be a man in the midst of it. When a man yields to God in difficulty, he turns weakness into strength.

". . . I fear no evil for thou art with me" (Ps. 23:4). "And [God] said, 'My Grace is sufficient for you, for my power is made perfect in weakness . . . '" (2 Cor. 12:9).

When a Man's a Fool

When is a man a fool? It's bad enough to be called that by a man . . . infinitely worse to be labeled a fool by God. There are times when God does do this—times when a man merits this serious rebuke.

"The fool says in his heart, 'There is no God.'" He is a fool because he operates strictly contrary to the evidence . . . evidence without and within: the evidence of design and purpose in nature—the evidence of conscience!

It is irrational not to believe in God because the universe cries out with testimony from every nook and cranny that God is. It would be easier to believe a watch could happen without a watchmaker than that this world came into being without a designer.

The atheist has a faith. He believes in no-god. He believes

in Nothing. Nothing is his god. What a terrible emptiness to live a life predicated on this kind of faith. No wonder such a faith could breed communism.

When Jesus finished His Sermon on the Mount, He said, "Every one then who hears these words of mine and does them will be like a wise man who built his house upon the rock; and the rain fell, and the floods came, and the winds blew and beat upon that house, but it did not fall, because it had been founded on the rock. And every one who hears these words of mine and does not do them will be like a foolish man who built his house upon the sand; and the rain fell, and the floods came, and the winds blew and beat against that house, and it fell; and great was the fall of it!" (Matt. 7:24–27).

There is only one adequate foundation of life: obedience to Jesus Christ. The man who refuses the counsel of Christ is a fool in God's estimation. Build your house on sand and the whole superstructure collapses in the storm.

Then there's the story of the wealthy farmer. He had a bumper crop—barns already full. He tore them down and built greater to house his increase. Then he relaxed, and comforted his soul with these words: "Soul . . . take your ease, eat, drink, be merry . . . you have ample goods laid up for many years . . . " (Luke 12:18–19).

Nothing to worry about . . . he thought! *But God called him a fool.* "Fool! This night your soul is required of you. . . ." He'd taken care of everything . . . except the one inevitable emergency—death!

Foresight and vision only for the materialism of life. Utterly blind and unprepared for the deeper things—things of the spirit. What a treacherous distortion of values. Satiated for time . . . barren for eternity!

Intelligent planning for life involves planning for the one

great emergency. And God has provided adequately for this need of man in the person of Jesus Christ His Son. Faith in Christ guarantees a man's future.

"Every one who calls upon the name of the Lord will be saved!" (Rom. 10:13).

Why Pray?

If God is all-powerful—and all wise . . . and if He knows what He's going to do anyway—why pray? What rational place does prayer have in the universe? Plenty of men question this way, and see no real point in prayer.

There are two extremes to which a government can go: tyranny or paternalism. And sometimes both may be practiced by one government. Either or both destroy human nature by failing to take into consideration the basic dignity of man and his inalienable rights.

Tyranny suppresses and enslaves, treating human nature like chattel having no inherent value—it is worthwhile only as it serves the ends of the tyrant.

Paternalism also suppresses and enslaves—if in a more subtle and damning way. It destroys initiative and self-confidence and incentive. The government provides all that is needed. And in so doing makes the recipient of the dole a complete slave—utterly dependent on the system that supports him.

The ideal government works with the consent of the governed. Whatever form it takes, it recognizes the dignity of man—the inherent worth of the individual. It encourages and rewards initiative. That government is best which governs by the suffrage of the people.

This is because God created man with personal dignity: to be free—to make his own choices and bear the consequences. *He did not make man a puppet!* God created man with incentive and initiative. And He does not intend to destroy either of these qualities that make a man a man!

Therefore God will not rule without the consent of those over whom He rules! God is neither tyrant or paternalist! He will not force obedience involuntarily, nor will He destroy man by putting him on the dole.

This is the kind of world in which we live. This is the divine economy! And because of this any government that tyrannizes or paternalizes must ultimately fail. God loves man—will govern him only as man consents . . . will grant him only that of His gifts man seeks.

And this is the point of prayer! By prayer man consents to the rule of God in his life. By prayer man seeks God's will and yields to it. By prayer man asks God for that which he knows he needs and can receive only from God.

Prayer is man's way of consenting to the government of God. Prayer is the means whereby man seeks the will and way of God. Prayer is that contact man has with the heavenly Father to satisfy the deepest needs of his life.

And a man is truly a man only when he is governed by God—only as he is in fellowship with God. Ruled by himself—or any other—he is less than a man. Out of touch with God he is sub-human! Man out of touch with God is like a fish out of water. He's not "at home" until he's right with God!

"Ask, and it will be given you; seek, and you will find; knock, and it will be opened to you . . . " (Luke 11:9).

Saint or Sinner?

"I don't figure I live a good enough life to call myself a Christian," said a man to me. He was an outstanding, intelligent, successful businessman.

But he was only half right! He was right when he declared that he could not live a good enough life. No one can! The Bible declares all the way through this inadequacy of man to live as he should.

But he was wrong in what he meant by what he said. What he meant was that no man has the right to call himself a Christian *until* he lives a perfect life. If that were true only one man in history could claim to be a Christian—Jesus Christ Himself.

The idea behind this man's statement is that a man becomes a Christian only after he has somehow lived up to some impossible ethical or moral standard. Until a man can maintain this perfection (according to this way of thinking) he's a hypocrite to call himself Christian.

On the surface this sounds humble, but yet underneath it's the kind of pride that's at the bottom of most of man's trouble. Actually this attitude is a kind of hypocrisy. If a man really believed he could not live good enough, he'd be the first to believe the Bible and follow Jesus Christ.

This is the central theme of the Bible: There is something fundamentally wrong and basically weak about human nature. This weakness causes a man to do the things he doesn't want to do, and keeps him from living the way he should. In short man is a sinner! The Bible states this quite bluntly!

And for this reason God sent His Son into the world—the "Lamb of God" to take away sin. This is the good news—the gospel: though man is a sinner, God has sent Christ, who is the Remedy for sin! The gospel is "the power of God" . . . power to change a man—make him right!

Now as a matter of fact the only people who refused to listen to Jesus Christ were those religious men who felt they could live good enough without any help. It was this attitude that finally led to the crucifixion.

They criticized Christ for fraternizing with sinners. He replied: "Those who are well have no need for a physician, but those who are sick. [The Son of Man has] not come to call the righteous, but sinners to repentance!"

The point is this: Christ will help the man who really thinks he's not able to live good enough. But when a man says this and at the same time will not listen to Jesus Christ, it's a fair guess he really thinks he's doing pretty well!

A Christian is not one who lives a perfect life. He's one who admits his need—and lets Christ help him. The sinner is the one who really qualifies for God's help. Men who don't think they're sinners won't bother!

"The Son of Man is come to seek and to save those who are lost . . ."

Future Guaranteed

"There's nothing I fear worse than going down a dark hallway and finding no door at the end!"

Thus a young insurance executive expressed his fear of discovering, when he was forty-five, that he had been in the wrong business.

He kept what he called an "open mind" to be sure he did not get in a rut that led to a dead end just when he ought to expect the payoff to begin.

This thinking makes sense (What's worse than investing life and energy in something that doesn't prove out in the end?), but with this fear it is impossible for a man to let himself out to really do a job that will assure a payoff.

There is no more pathetic tragedy than the might-have-been . . . the man who spent himself at the wrong task—a square peg in a round hole! Just when some legitimate returns should be coming in he discovers he's been barking up the wrong tree . . . going down the wrong road that leads to . . . nowhere!

It is great when young fellows can figure this out early enough. Pity the man who carries on with blinders because he won't think—or can't . . . or because he's willing to settle for mediocrity and the second best.

Then he reaches forty-five and finds himself at the end of the hallway with no door. All he can do is dig in and make the best of a second-rate finish.

This is the tragedy of tragedies . . . because it is utterly unnecessary!

No man has to accept the second best for himself! There's a place in the sun for every man and it's his own fault if he misses it!

God has a plan for your life! And when a man's life is God-planned, he'll find the place where he belongs—the place where the payoff is right . . . if he consents to God's will! He'll find the place of fulfillment: a productive, fruitful, completely satisfying life now and forever . . . *providing he lets God lead!*

God's plan for your life is perfect—down to the microscopic details. If you miss it, don't blame God. A man must look into his own heart for the explanation. God is not reluctant to lead. He promises to direct the steps of any man who submits to His direction!

Nothing delights God more than to lead a man. This is expressly declared and continually ratified in the Bible. God leads the man who seeks His guidance—yields to His rule of love!

God's plan means complete and perfect fulfillment of the man: Every talent with which he is endowed—every built-in aptitude gets its proper play. A man becomes himself in the fullest sense of the word when his life is God led. Therefore let go . . . and let God!

"The steps of a man are from the LORD . . . (Ps. 37:23).

The New Man

A thing that often brings discouragement, sometimes despair, to the Christian man is the apparent futile struggle to live a Christian life. He's anxious to be a Christian. He's got it in his heart to emulate Jesus Christ—to demonstrate Christian virtue . . . but try as he will his efforts are continually met by defeat and failure.

This frustration is a double unfortunate when one realizes that such a futile struggle is not only unnecessary . . . but it is contrary to the Scriptures.

A man begins to be a Christian when he recognizes need in his life that he himself is unable to meet—when he realizes that God has already provided a solution in the Person of His Son, Jesus Christ; and that there is something workable—something relevant in Christ's cross and resurrection.

Acknowledging his need and his inability to do anything about it, he turns to Christ. This act of receiving Christ, or believing in Christ, marks the start of the Christian life. But it's only the beginning.

The Christian man has two natures. The old nature that he has had from birth, and the new nature that God gives him at the new (spiritual) birth. New birth occurs at the moment a man asks God to come into his life.

Growing up spiritually is a matter of feeding this new nature that it may become strong and virile. Frustration comes when the Christian man struggles to discipline and control the old nature, trying to make it something it can never become. Of course, it's a futile task!

Much so-called Christian growth is nothing more than the development and refinement of native virtues . . . dusting off and polishing up the old nature. This may produce some pretty good imitations occasionally, but it's a far cry from the real thing!

Christian maturity is effortless on the part of the Christian. It is the "fruit of the Spirit." This "fruit" does not come by grunting and groaning any more than an apple tree produces apples by struggle. Apples come because the life of the apple is in the tree!

The effort in the Christian life comes at the point of feeding the new nature on the Word of God—nourishing it by prayer, Christian fellowship, and service. Discipline is at the point of submission to the rule of God in the heart—yielding to His will—renouncing one's own way.

When a man lets God have His way in his life, the beauty of God's character will be manifest in that man! The body is the "temple of the Holy Spirit" and He will express His nature—Christ-like nature—in and through the man who allows Him to reign in his body!

This is the secret of satisfaction in the Christian life. Not struggle to make something of the old nature . . . but walking in obedience to Jesus Christ, who actually entered your life when you asked Him to!

"I have been crucified with Christ; it is no longer I who live, but Christ who lives in me . . . " (Gal. 2:20).

Epitaph

"He was a good man." "He never harmed anyone."

Every once in awhile a pastor is called upon to conduct the funeral of a man who has not been in church for years. Aware of this, and usually quite sensitive about it, the family makes every effort to present the man in a favorable light to the minister. Sort of a vindication for him.

In his defense, one of two things (or both) is invariably said: "He was a good man," or "He never did any harm to anybody."

At such a time a pastor must be kind to those who sorrow, and he must do his best to make the funeral a blessing while at the same time keeping faith with his conscience and honesty.

But there are two questions he is tempted to ask at times: "He was a good man—but good for what?" "He has never harmed anyone—has he ever done anything for anyone?"

Good—but good for what? That's the point! Just being good is not sufficient. A man ought to be good for something!

There is nothing more pathetic than a man preoccupied with his own goodness. Goodness that ends here is useless. It might as well not have been. Has goodness blessed? Has it helped the world be a better place? This makes sense!

Nor is it enough just not to harm. (How sad to be able to

credit a man only for what he has *not* done.) Has the man done anything for anybody? He hasn't done any harm, but has he done anything else: for his neighbors—his community—his country—his God?

A man is born into a world filled with opportunity. It's all here for him. God has seen to that! All the raw materials to make life worthwhile. And a man is accountable to God as to what use he makes of these resources—how he invests them—whether or not he is productive!

Simply to be good, or to be harmless, is a million miles from the mark of any man who is worth his weight in more than sawdust! Taking these resources, developing them to the glory of God and the benefit of others, so that at life's end there is a deposit of goodness—of blessing—of inspiration—of strength—of beauty that benefits the world . . . that is living!

"He who had received the five talents went at once and traded with them; and he made five talents more. So also, he who had the two talents made two talents more. But he who had received the one talent went and dug in the ground and hid his master's money" (Matt. 25:16–18).

And the Lord blessed the man with five talents—and the man with two . . . but He sorely rebuked the man who had hidden his talent . . . who simply kept it and did not make it productive.

Strength of Faith

The strength of faith is not faith itself (how much a man has). The strength of faith is the faithfulness of God!

This is the backbone of faith: a God who is absolutely

dependable—absolutely trustworthy . . . who never fails—who never changes—who never backs down on His promises . . . for whom nothing is too hard or impossible!

He is never taken by surprise—never under the pressure of emergency—never "in the dark" about His world or His people. He knows "the end from the beginning." He has not abdicated! He is in control—on His throne!

Furthermore, He is interested in us—in each man. He has concern for our needs. He is always near—always available—always more willing to bless than we are to be blessed. There is no reluctance with God!

Faith in and of itself is powerless. If faith does not rest in a faithful object, then faith will be meaningless.

Trust in that which is not trustworthy leads to disappointment. Invest in a venture that fails, regardless of how much faith you have in it, you will lose your investment. The only thing that makes faith valid is that in which faith is put! The object of faith is the thing . . . not faith itself!

So it is in the Christian life. Not great faith . . . but faith in a great God! Emphasis is on God—not on faith!

A man examines himself introspectively—looks inward at his faith to see how much is there—and becomes discouraged by what he sees. Concerned, he tries to "have faith" or "get faith" somehow. Introspection becomes a vicious spiral that leads to blacker and blacker discouragement.

What's happening is that he is becoming preoccupied with faith, which by itself is nothing whatever . . . and is forgetting the God of his faith.

Faith must not look inward to itself. Faith in faith is nothing! Like adding zero to zero without an integer. No matter how many zeros you add, the sum total is zero! Put an integer in front, and they add up!

73

Faith does not accomplish anything. God accomplishes it! Faith is the means whereby a man agrees with God—yields to God—obeys God! Submit to God by faith and through the door of faith God works in your life!

It is not that God cannot work without our faith. God is never handicapped! But God will not work without our faith. He's made it this kind of a world.

The secret of strong and healthy faith is constant cultivation of the presence of God in Christ in the life. Center your attention—your affection—on Him, and faith comes along withoutany difficulty. Think of God—not faith!

". . . [Abraham] did not weaken in faith . . . fully convinced that God was able to do what he had promised" (Rom. 4:21).

Horse Sense

There's more to this matter of "horse sense" than some might think.

In one respect at least a man is like a horse. He's not really of much practical use until he's broken!

A wild horse out on the mesa may be thrilling to watch, but he never carries a rider or pulls a load. All his energy, his strength, his speed, and his beauty are wasted . . . until he's broken.

A man is that way too. He may be quite exciting and attractive when wild and untamed . . . but he doesn't pull a load! He needs to be broken for harness! He may hold great promise: purebred pedigree—intelligence—strength—drive, but until he's broken, all these qualities are dissipated.

That's the point of a broken spirit; not that a man's will is smashed, but that it is channeled, directed to useful and productive ends! Man broken God's way is man with all his qualities under control!

A friend in the San Joaquin Valley owns one of the finest Arabian stallions in the world. He's beautiful, intelligent, fast, and alert. It's a treat just to watch him. He's been broken! He's delicately sensitive and responsive to the slightest command.

He hasn't lost any of his brilliance or speed or strength or intelligence. It's all there—under control! What a stallion . . . kingly!

Being broken conditions a man for success! The man who gets there without it spoils instead of maturing. Success goes to his head, not his heart. He gets "too big for his pants." Little man in a big place . . . and everyone knows it!

The thing to see is that God orders—or allows things in a man's life that are designed to break him! "Whom the Lord loves—he chastens."

Behind this breaking process, this chastening, this discipline, is the infinite wisdom—the changeless love—the perfection of a heavenly Father who never makes a mistake! He knows just how much a man can bear, just how hot and how radical and how severe the tempering process needs to be!

He loves enough not to stop the discipline short of its perfect goal . . . never to let it go beyond what a man can endure. He knows a man's metal!

Some keen disappointment, heartbreaking tragedy, unexpected reversal in the Father's love and providence are steps to maturity and supreme usefulness!

"The sacrifice acceptable to God is a broken spirit: a broken and contrite heart, O God, thou will not despise" (Ps. 51:17).

Bona Fide

Look for the soundest investment—with the greatest security—paying the highest dividend—over the longest period of time—with the richest incidental rewards . . . what do you think it is?

It is not real estate, or government bonds, or business and industry. It is investment in life . . . life dedicated to the kingdom of God enterprise!

By any test you make, investment in human life brings the maximum satisfaction in time and eternity. Nothing else is so rewarding! The returns are measureless. The dividends are beyond our apprehension!

Once on the Breakfast Club broadcast, the head of the Shrine projects for crippled children was being interviewed. He told how the Shriners spend millions annually on this project. "We do not look on it as an expense costing too much—we regard it as an investment in the future of America."

Not expense . . . investment! That's sanity! That's wisdom. That makes sense! They simply can't lose on that!

Let's face it! How a man spends his money is the most accurate, penetrating index into that man's character. This is true of an organization . . . or a nation as well! It's true of business and industry too!

According to the U.S. Dept. of Commerce, the average earnings of every man, woman, and child in the U.S. in 1951 was $1,584. Their total average contribution to all religious and welfare projects for the same year was $26.14. That's less than 2%. And the government allows a deduction of 20%!

If everyone had given only 10%, which is the Bible norm for God's people, the average would have been $158.40. What a difference!

The Wall Street Journal shows that although a corporation may deduct 5% of its earnings for religious and charitable gifts, the average corporation gives less than 1%. And only four-hundreths of one percent is given to religious work!

"The members of the Communist party in the U.S. gave $50 to propagate their cause for every $1 Americans of all denominations gave for all religious purposes in one year." (*Christian Life* Magazine) fifty to one!

Corporations investing less than 1%—individuals less than 2%. And both have a tremendous stake involved. Is it any wonder we are losing the very thing that makes individual freedom and corporate enterprise possible?

"Will a man rob God?" "Give and it shall be given unto you. . ."

Bottleneck

One reason some men never prosper is because they cannot be trusted with prosperity! This is not the only reason . . . but it's a very significant one!

The way they use their money—what little they have—is the thing that's "bottlenecking" a greater flow of it through their hands.

A man gets the idea it's nobody's business but his how he spends his money! He earns it by hard work . . . he's the one to decide how it'll be used. He'll "do as he pleases" with his money.

But nine times out of ten when a man has this attitude toward his money, he leaves God out entirely. He ignores God's priority in life. He has no sense of his obligation to God in finances.

The way he figures it, he's got a hard enough time making ends meet as it is. In fact, he doesn't make it. Every month living demands more than he's making. Wages don't seem to have the same elasticity as cost of living. With the result that, financially speaking, he's always behind the eight ball!

Naturally it seems perfectly logical for him to bypass the church in the matter of giving. Perhaps a dollar or so a week— sort of a token gift—but that's the end of the matter. And this makes good sense to the man!

But it's not good sense! It's a distorted sense of values! It's the sole reason some men do not prosper more; the reason they've always got a struggle on their hands. They work hard . . . but they refuse to acknowledge God and His lordship!

Their thinking runs along this line: When I'm making enough to cover all my legitimate needs, pay my debts, and have something left over, then it's time to think about God in finances. "Surely God expects me to pay my debts!" Sounds sensible . . .

But every man has a debt to God! What this man is really doing is putting God last! After everything else, then God comes in for a share! Which attitude—if it were not so pathetically tragic—would be laughable! Everything is God's in the first place!

First things first makes sense to every thinking man! God's place is first! If God is not first, then belief in God is meaningless. Faith is a travesty. The Bible nonsense!

The easiest time to put God first is when a man's wages are small, because systematic giving is the Bible pattern. The first tenth is the Bible system! The first tenth belongs to God! Obviously systematic giving becomes more difficult as wages increase. Time to begin is when a man is worst off. Put God first then . . . and keep God first always!

"Will a man rob God? Yet you are robbing me. But you say, 'How are we robbing thee?' In your tithes and offerings. You are cursed with a curse, for you are robbing me; the whole nation of you. Bring the full tithes in . . . and put me to the test says the LORD—if I will not open the windows of heaven—and pour down for you an overflowing blessing" (Mal. 3:8–10).

Providence

God has angles a man would never think of! Ways of going at a problem—working it out—that would never occur to us.

Because He sees the end from the beginning . . . and all the stages in between. Like an architect, who sees the finished product.

We see just a part of the process: scaffolding—loose bricks and boards—no semblance of order. Being so involved in the process—so close to the thing—we fail to get the perspective on it.

God sees it from above. The whole pattern at once! He knows things that are obscure—or completely unknown to us. Furthermore, God is always in control! He never lets go—never relinquishes His rule!

God's man learns to see things God's way! God is the major factor in his calculations! He knows he can count on God's utter dependability! He reckons on His never-failing presence . . . His omnipotence!

To him God is the God of creation! He is the God of the impossible! Nothing is too hard for Him!

God can begin with nothing—begin with zero—and produce! Man can invent . . . only God can create! Man must begin with something—to produce something. Not God! The Hebrew word for create (bara) means to "make something out of nothing" (Gen. 1:1). God can start from scratch!

Measure God by our standards—drag Him down to our level—whittle Him down to our size . . . we end up with a God who is as helpless as we are! We figure He's got to have something to begin with. We search desperately amidst our troubled circumstances—to find something God can begin with.

If we find something, we muster a glimmer of hope. If we find nothing, we get nervous—begin to despair—forget He is the God of creation.

Faith in God is faith in God. Regardless of circumstances, no situation is hopeless, no condition impossible with God! God is God. He never has been—never will be—at the mercy of circumstances. He rules them—orders them!

The secular man looks around at his circumstances, seeking a way of escape. The Christian man looks up—to God! In a corner? No way to turn? No way out? When things look blackest—look up! God is able!

"All things work together for good to them who love God, who are the called according to his purpose . . . " (Rom. 8:28 KJV). "Commit your way to the LORD; trust in him, and he will act" (Ps. 37:5).

A Man's Man!

"A man's man!" You often hear that with reference to someone who has qualified in some way among his friends. What does it mean? When is a man "a man's man"?

It certainly doesn't have to do with bulk—broad shoulders—bulging biceps—massive chest. Often men with these qualifications are like clods. They can be pushed around with ease . . .

Nor does it have to do with size. Which is probably an accident of birth. Many men who stand head and shoulders above their fellows are whipped over and over again in the battles that really matter.

You judged beef on the hoof by bigness—sheer bulk . . . but you don't pick a man that way!

Some of the biggest men are like putty in the midst of the crowd. They're nothing more than tools. They don't think for themselves—they let someone else do their thinking. They're just dead weight—going downstream with the crowd.

They look big outwardly, but inside they're jelly fish. They could slug it out with a man—like brute beasts in a jungle! But they lose every battle that involves principle!

There's something more to a man than bone and muscle.

A man's man *dares to stand for a principle*—when the whole world stands against him. He dares to fight the current—dares to uphold the right against all odds. He doesn't yield easily to the whims of the crowd.

He's got a flash-point against sin! He dares not to laugh at an obscene story. He is indignant when men use the name of Christ in cursing—smear it around with filthy banter—lewd jokes.

He has the courage to guard what is sacred. He dares to profess love for God in the midst of a materialistic, secular crowd that might jeer. He stands against the awful tide of cheap tawdry conversation when men gather.

He is ruled by principle—when most men are governed by expediency! He isn't sucked in by the stupid philosophy: "Everybody's doing it!"

God give us men! Real men! With character—inner poise . . . who offer stubborn resistance against the flood of moral laxity—irreligion—loose living—luxury-loving, comfort-seeking, drunkenness that is saturating and destroying our society!

Size really makes very little difference! It's what's in the head—and *especially in the heart* that counts! Strength of will—not muscle . . . purpose—not brawn . . . the ability to finish—to see a thing through!

"No man having put his hand to the plow—and turning back . . . is fit for the kingdom of God!"

Saved

Strangely enough, one of the most wonderful words in the English language is a word many fear. Though it brings comfort and confidence and assurance it is offensive to many. Some have tried to boycott it.

It is not a complicated word invented by theologians. It is a common biblical word. Though men have tried synonyms to take its place none is adequate. None say it quite as well as this word!

The word is *saved!*

Jesus said this is what He had come to do. This was the heart of the apostolic message. It sums up the whole divine program in the world. It is the whole point of Jesus' coming: His life, death, resurrection . . . and His coming again! It is the theme of the Bible from Genesis to Revelation.

Millions of men and women testify to the experience of

"being saved." They are not boasting! They are bearing witness to something that has happened to them—a work of divine grace in their lives. They actually have an inner assurance of their eternal well-being.

The saved man gives no credit to himself—puts no confidence in himself. He simply trusts Christ! He believes in the redemptive work of Christ—in the word of His promise. He is not proud . . . just grateful!

It is not conceit when a man believes he is saved. Nor is it humility not to believe it! If Jesus Christ is to be trusted . . . if the Bible is to be taken seriously . . . then men ought to be aware of being saved. Men ought to glorify God because of it!

A man says he believes the teaching of Jesus, but he does not know that he's saved—that no one can know. This is a contradiction!

To say one cannot be sure of his salvation is to say one cannot be sure of Christ and His promises. This is to dishonor the Savior who laid down His life that men might be saved.

To be saved means exactly what it says: It means to be *safe!* It means to be safe from the long-term consequences of sin. It means to be safe from the penalty of sin. It means to be safe eternally! This is the only true security!

It does not mean to be sinless. It does not mean the saved man no longer sins or fails. But it does mean that God has done something in his life that guarantees his eternal welfare. It does mean he has repented and asked God's forgiveness and help.

It means a man is trusting the grace of God, that he has received the gift of grace, which is eternal life through Jesus Christ. He is not working for it . . . he has received it! He already has it! It's a gift!

Any man can be saved who wants to be. God loves all men.

The man who is unsaved is the man who refuses the gift of God.

"God so loved the world that he gave his only Son, that whoever believes in him should not perish but have eternal life" (John 3:16).

Leadership

One of the most desperate needs in America today is solid, dependable, strong leadership! Daily we see the tragedy of weak men in important places—little men in big jobs—who inevitably drag the job down to their size! Too often we've been sending boys to do a man's work!

Business—industry—government—labor—the church—education . . . all are starving for leadership. And so few men are willing to pay the price!

What qualifies a man for leadership? First of all he must be a good follower. That man is utterly unqualified who has never learned to follow. He who cannot take orders will never be in a position to give them!

The man who has not first learned to obey as a subordinate will never command obedience as a leader!

The leader must accept responsibility. He'll see a job done whether it's his to do or not. He'll do it for the sake of getting it done! He'll not be continually complaining: "I'm not paid to do this," or "This isn't my job!"

He'll accept 'round-the-clock pressure, because the leader doesn't have "hours." He doesn't watch the clock! His responsibility is with him constantly: eating—playing—sleeping—it's always there, always on his mind! He can't shake it at 5:00 p.m. or on Saturday and Sunday.

He must be willing to bear others' burdens. He cannot be indifferent to them! He must absorb some of their shock, lift some of their load, share some of their trials, face some of their problems . . .

He may in fact find himself so busy with their problems that he'll have little if any time to think about and solve his own.

A leader must lead, not follow the crowd. Things that are right for others may not be right for him. He sets standards—doesn't conform to the status quo.

He looks ahead—beyond things as they are—to what he can make them. He must look past disappointment that would frustrate a lesser man, plow through discouragement and failure to achievement!

He must be able to see a thing through, in spite of defeat . . . to finish the thing begun, even when he's lost interest. He must plug along when there is no inspiration. He needs sheer, dogged endurance which separates men from boys.

Above all he needs patience! He must put up with little people who oppose him, who knife him in the back, who have petty, backbiting attitudes. He must be patient in set-backs and reverses, when selfish interests invade and upset and bog down. He must be patient in the midst of a thousand-and-one-things that drive other men crazy—make them quit. This is the price of leadership!

"He who seeks his life, loses it . . . he who loses his life, finds it!" "It is required in stewards that a man be found faithful. . ."

God's Will Involves Schedule

Three things are involved in the will of God! Three things a man must take into consideration when he decides to line up with God's plan and purpose.

Understanding these is the key to personal power—maturity—freedom—efficiency—and maximum productivity.

They are: *product, process,* and *schedule.* The end, the means, and the time involved. God's will includes *what* He intends to accomplish, *how* He intends to do it, and *when* it will be finished.

God has a perfect plan for your life. This involves a perfect goal, a perfect process whereby this goal is to be realized, and a perfect schedule for its operation and completion.

Most of us see the point of being committed to the *what* of God's will. But we get all messed up and confused when it comes to the *how* and the *when!*

We are willing for God's will to be done, but we are often unwilling to submit to the process involved . . . and usually are very impatient with the time it takes.

Take for example the matter of humility: the average Christian man would like to be humble. He recognizes humility as an excellent grace—a virtue to be cherished. He dislikes the conceited man—abhors conceit in himself.

But there's only one way to be humble, and that's to be humiliated! Humility is the product of which humiliation is the process! Humility that is put on or acted out is hypocritical. Fake humility is worse than conceit!

The only humility worthwhile is that which has been worked out in a man's life by the process of humiliation. This produces a genuine, deeply humble man! And this takes time too. But it's worth it!

Here's a man who lacks patience. Ashamed of himself, he prays to be a patient man. God answers by sending along a cranky neighbor—or a stubborn problem—or some other distressing thing . . . designed to develop patience.

The man balks! He wants to be patient, but he's unwilling to undergo the process by which patience is worked into his life. This takes time too!

God's will includes all three: the what—the how—and the when. These three are inseparably linked together. Submitting to God's will means submitting to the process and the schedule as well as the product.

Of course it's difficult. But a man isn't worth his weight in sawdust who tries to escape the difficulties that build character—that make the man! These things build the men who build empires.

". . . the testing of your faith produces steadfastness. And let steadfastness have its full effect, that you may be perfect and complete, lacking in nothing" (James 1:3, 4).

Real God

What is God like?

Through the centuries men have struggled to find the answer to that question. And far too often their quest has ended in failure and despair!

Men realize instinctively that it is important to know God—they never seriously doubt that God is there—somewhere . . . but where? How can God be found? How can God be known?

Of course there have been those in every generation who have totally disregarded the abundant evidence on every hand, and have denied the existence of God.

Which is interesting. Because if there were not a God to deny, the arguments of the atheist would be ridiculous and laughable. No one would take him seriously.

The only thing that saves the atheist's self-respect is the fact that there is a God against whom his struggle is a real one! The atheist is not shadow boxing. If God did not exist, the atheist would not be taken any more seriously than a man who vociferously tried to prove there is no Santa Claus.

God is there, to be sure. No one honest with himself in his heart will deny this. But where? And what is God like? How can He be known?

Many failing to find God outside themselves invent a god. But this invented god has never been quite satisfactory. After all, it doesn't make sense for a man to bow down and worship that which he himself creates.

The New Testament has a clear answer to this problem! And multiplied millions of men and women through the ages have discovered that God is no mystery at all. He can be known! He can be as real as a friend!

The answer is Jesus Christ! God is like Jesus Christ! Get to know Jesus Christ and you'll find that God is a reality in your experience.

This is not something to argue about! This is something to experience! As long as men insist on arguing with Jesus Christ, they will never get to know God. But if a man will honestly try Jesus Christ, he'll be in for the most important discovery of his life!

What can a man lose by giving Christ a chance? If He is not real . . . if He is not God . . . a man will soon discover that. The tragedy is in the man who won't try Jesus Christ—just argues about Him.

If you have never admitted Christ into your life, open your heart to Him. Ask Him to come in. Tell Him you are willing to follow Him—obey Him. You'll find how near God is to you—how willing He is to come into your life, to make it everything it ought to be. Try Jesus Christ now!

"To all who received him . . . he gave power to become children of God . . . " (John 1:12).

History in Miniature

Mark 12:1–11 contain a parable portraying graphically human nature as God sees it. It is a vivid, penetrating description of this world the way it really looks to God.

The Lord tells the story of a man who planted a vineyard. He made the usual preparations involved in such a venture, leased it out to tenants, and departed for a far country.

In time he sent a servant to collect his portion of the fruit of the vineyard. But the tenants beat the servant and sent him away empty-handed. More servants were dispatched, and each in his turn received the same—or worse treatment.

Finally the owner of the vineyard sent his only son, feeling the tenants would reverence him, and give him his father's due.

But the tenants heaped the final infamy on the owner. They killed his son!

That is the story of human nature. God set man in a beautiful world, with every conceivable thing for his pleasure. Man was to cultivate it—enjoy it.

This is the essence of sin—that man stubbornly refuses to acknowledge God's ownership of the world. Man turned from God—went his own way—lived as though God were unimportant. Man prostituted his tenancy—spent his money—planned his life—without a serious thought of his duty to God!

God sent many servants to His prodigal world, but always the story was the same. The prophets were stoned or killed, and their message was largely disregarded. God's right of eminent domain was utterly ignored!

Finally, in the fullness of time, God sent His only Son—the Lord Jesus Christ. Surely man would reverence Him. But human nature put Him on a cross!

Twenty centuries have passed, and still men are crucifying Christ today! Not with crown of thorns, or spittle, or ridicule so much, but with their condescension, their patronage, or by utterly ignoring Him. This is the cruelest kind of crucifixion!

When you stop to think about it, this is the worst thing that can be said about human nature. This is the worse indictment . . . it crucified the Son of God. And still does today!

The clearest truth in the New Testament is that God expects men to reverence His Son . . . that rejection of the Son is rejection of the Father! Men who refuse to worship Jesus Christ prove their antipathy to God Himself!

This is the clue to the world's salvation, to turn again to God, to recognize His Son, to acknowledge His Lordship with obedience and faith. "He that dishonors me dishonors my Father; he that honors me, honors my Father also."

Due for Crackup?

Quit taking yourself so seriously! No man is as important as he thinks he is! Quit kidding yourself! Relax! You're heading for a tailspin!

There is a peculiar kind of pride that grips a man in these pressure days. Men worship power—prominence—influence—drive. It gets some men and drags them to an early grave.

A fellow gets to thinking he's indispensable to his work. Feels it just won't go without him around to supervise—or do it himself. He kids himself into thinking he's just a hard worker. Actually, he's playing tricks on himself!

A man works eighteen hours a day, and brags about it! He wants it to be known! As though there's some unique virtue in working eighteen hours a day. Some men do this who produce very little . . . they're just hopelessly inefficient.

This guy says the work demands eighteen hours a day. Actually, that's an excuse—to cover up fear . . . the fear that he isn't really as important to his work as he wants to be.

Men like to think they are indispensable. It feeds the ego! It would be laughable if it were not so pitifully tragic. They slave away day after day—no time for God or Christ or the church, and little time for family and friends.

They're afraid to let go—afraid to take a vacation—afraid to relax. Afraid the business would get along without them . . . and they'd be shown up.

Men have cracked up over this. They kept driving until they were forced to take a rest. They were laid up for a week or so. To their amazement—and humiliation—business went on as usual. When they got back in harness they discovered the job hadn't suffered by their absence. It's a terrible blow to their ego—shattering to pride. Some men can't take it!

Make up your mind to this: the last man on earth to take too seriously is yourself. No man is indispensable to any job! The man who thinks he is, is in for a staggering blow.

It is absolutely ridiculous for good men to wear themselves out at an early age under this delusion. At bottom it is nothing more than pride. Which has ruined more men, disrupted more business, slowed down more production, wasted more energy than almost anything else.

God didn't make man to operate this way. He made man for fellowship with Himself. The man who has no time for God is a man fooling himself; he is cheating himself out of his most productive years. He reaches the point where he produces less per unit of energy, until he's actually going backwards.

"Everyone . . . is not to think of himself more highly than he ought to think . . ." (Rom. 12:3).

Faith Is Defensible

Christian faith is not what many think it is! No wonder men repudiate it, because they have such a distorted idea of what it is. At best their picture of faith is a horrible caricature.

"Faith is believing what you can't know," one college girl said. To her faith was a poor substitute for knowledge—a second-best thing. To her faith was short of a shot in the dark—a blind leap into the unknown. No wonder she rejected such a nebulous thing.

But faith is not believing what you can't know! You cannot

believe what you don't know! Faith without knowledge is impossible. Faith rests on knowledge! Knowledge is the foundation on which faith builds.

For instance—you don't trust a man you don't know. You don't commit your life to a physician who is unknown. You wouldn't engage an attorney you didn't know. You've got to know to trust! Faith begins with knowing.

This is the essence of Christian faith: it is rooted and grounded in a person! The Christian man has a personal acquaintance with Jesus Christ. To him Jesus is real—contemporary . . . not just a character in history.

Christianity is infinitely more than a creed—or ethics. It is to know Jesus Christ as a Friend—personally—intimately . . . not just about Him. Christian faith centers in Jesus Christ Himself!

Christian faith is not telling yourself something is true; making yourself believe it in order to make it true. Many look at it that way: Try hard enough and long enough to believe something . . . it'll be true for you.

Which is utterly ridiculous . . . and absolutely contrary to Christian faith! Any man with a rag of sense knows one cannot make a thing become true simply by believing it, no matter how intensely. Believing does not create that which is not! If a thing's not true, believing will never make it so!

Christian faith is believing a thing because it is true! It rests, not on ideas, but in events: Christ died for our sins, was buried, and rose again! That's the gospel!

Christian faith is provable—defensible! The test is whether or not it works. It is not true because it works, it works because it is true! Let the man who questions the validity of Christian faith run a test on it. Until he is willing to prove it, let him quit arguing. Let him hold his silence!

The Bible invites this: "Prove me now saith the LORD." "Taste and see that the LORD is good." Put Christ to the test! Try the promises of God. Prove for yourself faith is real—practical—workable.

Subtle Slavery

Do things belong to you . . . or do you belong to things? This is a basic issue in a man's life! It's the difference between a man's liberty and bondage . . . slavery or freedom! A man had better dare to examine his life at this point!

Some men don't possess their money. Their money possesses them. They began by making money and were blessed with a degree of prosperity. Then they got their eyes on money as more important than anything else . . . and ended up with money actually making them.

They thought they had wealth. In reality wealth had them! It was their idol—their god. And when money becomes a man's god, it inevitably destroys him!

God can't trust some men with prosperity. It would ruin them. They'd let money possess them, let it dictate to them, let it run their lives . . . until God wouldn't have a chance at their hearts. They'd let money take God's place in their lives.

Some men belong to everything. They belong to clubs, lodges, social sets, cliques. They let their jobs possess them, and these things run their lives unmercifully.

And these things run God right out of their lives! They don't have time for church—time for Bible reading and prayer—time for anything that is not prescribed by their club or lodge or social set. They become a tool of things!

Some men would like to quit drinking, but they can't! because group pressure dictates to them. Their lives are regimented by the group or social or business pressure. They follow the herd! They literally belong to these things—are possessed by them!

That is slavery of the worst kind! What a pity that big, good, intelligent men let themselves become enslaved by these things. What tragedy that such men become mastered by things, instead of mastering them!

But that's life! The man who is not mastered by God will be ruled by things—by mammon! There's no neutral ground. It's God or things! Each man chooses which it will be.

The important consideration is this: when things master a man, they enslave him. When God masters a man, He emancipates him. Jesus Christ died on a cross and rose again from the dead to liberate men. That's freedom!

When a man follows Christ—submits to Christ's rule in his life—he walks in an incredible liberty. He enjoys maximum freedom. Things belong to him—he does not belong to things!

"All things are yours, whether Paul or Apollos or Cephas or the world or life or death or the present or the future, all are yours; and you are Christ's; and Christ is God's" (1 Cor. 3:21–23).

Simplicity of Prayer

"Lord teach us to pray," asked the disciples of Jesus. They asked because they knew everything else about Him was due to His prayer life. His personal magnetism—His eloquence—His mastery of every situation—His power and strength.

95

Prayer was one of the most characteristic things about Him. He rose early, a great while before the day . . . He lingered in the late hours, after others had retired, to pray.

He maintained constant, conscious touch with His heavenly Father. This was the secret of His life. When we follow Him in His prayer life, we tap the secret of His resources. This is incumbent on every Christian man!

Some men do not pray because they think they do not know how. This is dead wrong. Prayer in its essence is as natural as breathing. It is as instinctive as a father-son relationship . . . as natural as turning to a kind father: seeking his counsel—his strength—his aid.

It is unfortunate—pitiable—when men make of prayer a peculiar religious exercise demanding special language and special forms; when they turn it into a formal, liturgical thing. That is appropriate for public prayer . . . it is foreign to real private, personal prayer.

Three things are paramount in prayer. They lead to simplicity—the key to real, effective, productive prayer. Prayer that will make a difference in your life—that will actually accomplish things!

First is this: God is your heavenly Father! "When you pray say 'Our father'" was the first instruction the Lord gave. God is not some far-off, unreal, ethereal abstraction. God is personal—like a father . . . with a father's love, a father's concern and interest, a father's willingness to help.

There is never any reluctance on God's part to bless men! Man's reluctance to come to God—seek His blessing and help—is the only thing that shuts out God's richest and best from him!

Second is: seek God's will and yield to His way! Let God's kingdom and righteousness be your primary interest. Do not be like a disobedient son in the home, in rebellion, wanting his own way, whining, pouting if he does not get it. Father knows best is the rule in the kingdom as well as at home.

Life will never be limited or confined, but enlarged and expanded for the man who submits to the rule of God in his life. This is the key to personal victory—maximum freedom—efficiency—productivity!

Third is this: pray in Christ's name. Not as some magic abracadabra, but approach God in the authority of Christ's sacrifice on the cross. By this sacrifice we have been reconciled to God. In this sacrifice we have freedom of access before God's throne. *Christ is the way to God!*

Take time daily to spend with your heavenly Father. You will reap rich, immeasurable dividends. "Men who kneel before God can stand up to anything!" Big men—strong men—come by prayer!

Men Should Pray

The average businessman's approach to Christianity is a practical one. He thinks in terms of tangibles—not in terms of abstractions.

Which is excellent, but it has its drawbacks! Because the "hardheaded" businessman (so called) often dismisses spiritual values as being utterly impractical and useless.

Take prayer for example. A man is apt to think of it as ethereal—a mystical exercise (of questionable value) for people who have nothing better to do. Certainly not for busy men in a hard, cold, calculating business world.

Which is unfortunate! Because rightly understood prayer is the most practical, relevant thing in life! In the Bible it is central—integral. It is to the spirit what distribution is to economics. Through prayer the resources of God are put to use. Without prayer these resources are available, but unappropriated!

Prayer is a businessman's greatest asset! The prayerless man is missing the boat! He's failing to come up to his best, failing to realize his top efficiency. The man who takes prayer seriously enjoys rich personal assets.

Humility. Not shallow—thin—pretense . . . but deep—basic—legitimate dependence on God. Absence of this is secularism—independence from God. The secular man writes God off . . .

No man is really great—or good—who is not humble before God! Without this man is a bore: he is cocky, unbearable, overbearing! Prayer settles a man into position, in honest dependence on God, recognizing God's place in the universe. Humility is strength under control!

Prayer gives a man strength! Endurance! Strength for emergencies, pressures, tensions. Prayer turns difficulty into opportunity . . . testing into tensile strength. It exploits trouble, uses it to build into a man resilience: prayer turns tragedy into triumph!

Prayer means power, in the sense of impact! The praying man has punch, drive, efficiency, striking force . . . a flash point. He is solid, sharp, keen. Man on his knees is man at his outside best.

God's wisdom comes through prayer. It means clearheaded, incisive decisions instead of confusion and foggy thinking. Prayer keeps a man from majoring in the minors—keeps him from concern for secondary matters and neglect of primary issues. Prayer gives a man proper perspective!

Whoever you are, whatever you do, take prayer seriously and you'll be a better man—more effective in your work, providing you put God first. Prayer is not in order that men may use God. It is that God may use men!

"Men ought always pray . . . and not give up!"—Jesus Christ.

Too Soon to Quit

It's not failing that's the sin . . . it's accepting failure as final that's the sin! No matter how often a man fails, he's not a failure until he takes it as final!

The man who goes places, who builds empires, is not the man who never fails. He is the man who never quits—no matter how many times he fails.

A young man jumps from one thing to another—one business to another—one project to another. Each time he fails he quits one thing and starts another. He takes every failure as final.

He keeps thinking he'll hit on something that will succeed. Every failure is proof to him he should be doing something else.

The trouble is not in his projects—not in what he's doing. The trouble is with the man himself! He'll keep on failing and keep on trying something new, never finding the combination for success.

Because the combination is within the man himself! He'll continue to fail in everything until he looks for the clue to success in himself, not in a new project!

The only men who never fail are the men who do nothing! There is certainly no virtue in not failing if a man does nothing at which to fail! Ridiculous as it may sound, some men would rather do nothing than risk failure. They'll never do anything either!

Many a race is won at the tape, in the last split-second! Many a fight is won in the last minute of the last round. No matter how often he's knocked down, the good fighter doesn't quit. Being knocked down isn't the sin . . . quitting is!

The man of achievement in any endeavor is the man who never takes failure as final! It is always part of the process. He makes every failure contribute to future success. He uses every failure as a stepping stone—not a stumbling block.

Every great man's life is dotted with failure. He learned from failure. Let failure season him—mature him—strengthen him! He didn't whine—didn't pout—didn't waste time on self-sympathy.

As Thomas Edison once said when an assistant urged him to quit after 1000 failures. "Why quit now—we know a 1000 things that won't work!"

It's always too soon to quit!

"And Jesus said to him, 'No one who puts his hand to the plow and turns back is fit for the kingdom of God'" (Luke 9:62).

The Core of Faith

There's a side to Christianity men do not take enough into consideration! Actually it's not a side . . . it's the center! It's the core—the heart of Christian faith. Take out this core and the whole structure caves in!

Without it there's no substance to Christianity—nothing to sink your teeth into . . . faith is unreal, impractical, ethereal. Might as well take any religion . . . or none at all!

Redemptive power is at the heart of Christian faith! This

is what makes it valid! The power of God—supernatural power— operating in and through man. The gospel is literally dynamite! It regenerates a man!

Men try every day to turn over a new leaf, to break old habits. That's reformation—the best man can do for himself. It's not enough. It may help a bit, but it falls short of Christianity!

Redemption is God's power—transforming the man! Jesus Christ doesn't repair the old nature or work it over. He creates a new nature and makes a new man! It's literally a new birth. Christ gets at the root of the trouble—human nature itself.

This is the fantastic thing about redemption. It takes the wrecks, the failures, the sins of the past, and blots them out as though they had never been. Gives a man a spanking fresh start!

Even if a man could begin to live a perfect life, never make another mistake, never commit another sin, he'd still have the past to pester him. Good living in the future will not wipe out the debt of the past.

Anymore than promising a bank never to be indebted to it in the future will cancel debts outstanding. They still must be paid! Man's effort at reform, even if successful, still falls tragically short of a real solution. But not redemption . . .

When Christ died on the cross He made a deposit of righteousness against man's sin. Not only is it sufficient for all man's present and future need . . . it is more than adequate to cover the guilt of the past—cancel the debt!

It is as though a man should go to your bank and deposit to your account 100 billion dollars (or more). Obviously that would take care of the past debts—and provide ample for future needs. That's the way the grace of God works! Incredible as it may seem, it's true!

This is the whole point of the Bible—the whole point of

Christ's life, death, resurrection. The whole point of the gospel. Yet there are men who reject it! Why? This is the best news a man can receive . . .

"Since all have sinned and fall short of the glory of God, they are justified by his grace as a gift, through the redemption which is in Christ Jesus, whom God put forward as an expiation (substitute) by his blood, to be received by faith" (Rom. 3:23–25).

Man Under Control

Have you ever stopped to consider how useless power is when it is not harnessed? Until it is brought under control—until it is channeled—it is utterly wasted!

In fact, it is not only useless, uncontrolled power can be tremendously destructive . . .

Take the billions of dollars damage done when the great rivers of this continent go on a rampage, overflow their banks and pour through dams and dikes.

Steam is useless and dangerous until it is guided into turbines. Then it becomes man's friend—works for him—drives his engines. For centuries men went without the incredible benefits of electricity. It was there all the time, but it was uncontrolled!

Human nature is useless too . . . and it can be very dangerous when it is uncontrolled! This is the most pathetic waste of all!

To be useful, human nature must be controlled! It must be directed—channeled—disciplined—if a man is to be worthwhile, efficient, productive!

The most pitiful tragedy in life is the "might-have-been." The powerful, splendid young man who had everything. With all of life before him and with almost unlimited potential . . . but he refused to yield to controls. He did as he pleased. His energy and ability were dissipated!

Skid row is filled with broken men without a goal or a purpose. Men who refused to be controlled and disciplined. Men who would not yield to authority. Pitiful—helpless—hopeless men!

Man who goes to the top does not do as he pleases! He submits to controls, to authority, to discipline! He brings his desires into line and channels his resources and strength into productive ends.

The stronger the man, the more necessary the controls! The more destructive he is without them!

The surest, steadiest, most dependable men are God-controlled men. Men who have submitted to the will of God in their lives. Men who take God seriously. Who not only believe in Him, but also live that way.

This is the highest goal—the most accurate direction a man can take: the glory of God! When this comes first it most thoroughly orients the man; it demands his best . . . gets it!

"Seek first his kingdom and his righteousness, and all these things shall be yours as well" (Matt. 6:33).

The Acid Test

The acid test of the Christian man is what he is, not what he does! What a man is when he's not trying or when he's off guard . . . when nobody's looking or when he's alone.

103

Christian character has to do with a man's nature, not his conduct!

Actually conduct doesn't prove anything. Because a bad man can order his conduct to impress people or gain their confidence, or to achieve an ugly purpose. He can pretend to be what he's not, and do great injury.

Furthermore the ethical norm for America is the Christian norm. Which means that even though he's not a Christian, the average American is guided by Christian principles.

Look at it this way: Not a man's actions but his reactions give the man away. This is the clue to the man he really is!

The average man would not murder, but he gets mad enough to murder. He wouldn't commit adultery, but he looks at a woman with lust in his heart.

Watch the businessman drive home from his office in the evening. Little things turn him into a savage animal. Let someone cut in on him in traffic. He'll boil, curse, explode— do everything he can to get even.

Normally he's mild-mannered, intelligent, and gentle, but he reacts to situations like a mad man.

What we need is a power that can control the passions that surge explosively beneath the surface. The lust, greed, and selfishness that lurks in a man's heart are the root of his trouble. These defeat the man!

High blood pressure, heart ailments, alcoholism . . . these and many others are the prices man pays for his sinful reactions to life, reactions over which he has no control. This is the pity—man at the mercy of himself. Victimized by himself!

For this reason the life surrendered to Jesus Christ means *victory!* Jesus Christ actually enters a man's life, gives him a new nature, and helps him react to life righteously rather than sinfully. He brings control at the point where man is uncontrolled!

The man yielded to the control of God in his life is the man with the bulge on his temptations—his reactions—himself. He's the man you want to be and ought to be!

". . . if you yield yourselves to anyone as obedient slaves, you are slaves of the one whom you obey, either of sin, which leads to death, or of obedience, which leads to righteousness" (Rom. 6:16).

This Is Life

Are you really alive . . . in the fullest sense of the word?

There are many kinds of life: Life as it is in a rock—as it is in a plant—as it is in an animal—as it is in man—as it is in God! Rock life—plant life—animal life—human life . . . and divine life!

Man, having been made in the image of God, is far more than an animal—more than just physical. Human life at its highest and best is spiritual! That man is only half human who lives at the level of the animal with bodily instincts . . . who satisfies only the fleshly desires . . . who obeys only the animal impulse!

Nor is he fully a man who disregards the life in the spirit—who lives simply at the human physical level, just a shade above the animal.

The man who is alive to the animal instincts, alive to the physical instincts, but dead spiritually, is not completely human. He is dead to God!

Death means separation: Physical death means separation from the flesh, from friends and loved ones, from this earth. *Spiritual death is separation from God!*

This explains the emptiness, the vacuum in so many men's souls. They are alive physically but not spiritually. They are alive to things on the horizontal level, but dead to the vertical relationship. Though they believe in God as an idea, He is not real to them or alive for them.

The process whereby one receives life is called birth. To have life one must be born with it. Life is not something a man can work to achieve. It is not something he can earn. Life is a gift! It can only be received!

Jesus Christ spoke to Nicodemus, one of the most religious, moral, intelligent men of the day: "Ye must be born again!" He did not need religion. He needed life—spiritual life. Life comes by birth. Therefore he needed to be born anew!

The true Christian man is *twice born*. Being Christian is infinitely more than mere morality. It is spirituality! The Christian man is one who has received the gift of eternal life. He is the man who is really living!

"This is the testimony, that God gave us eternal life, and this life is in his Son. He who has the Son has life; he who has not the Son of God has not life" (1 John 5:11, 12).

"To all who received him, who believed in his name, he gave power to become children of God; who were born, not of blood, nor of the will of the flesh nor of the will of man, but of God" (John 1:12, 13).

Steward or Squatter?

Life's finest, richest, purest blessing goes to the man who gives God first place in his financial program!

Jesus Christ said more about money than any other single thing. Because money is of first importance when it comes to a man's real nature.

Money is an exact index to a man's true character! Not how much he makes—but how he uses it and what he does with it after he makes it. This is the most accurate test for the man himself.

Some men live like "squatters" in this life. They take everything for granted! The wealth of the world belongs to the first man who gets it. Possession is everything!

The "squatter" has no sense of his responsibility to God. What's his is his . . . devil take the hindmost! He's a little dictator, a little god in his own little world.

Other men are stewards of their possessions. They recognize God's rights. They are conscious of an accountability to God that the "squatter" ignores!

They acknowledge God's right of "eminent domain" . . . they recognize this world as the divine preserve!

They brought nothing into this world. It was all here when they arrived! All the wealth and resources: sun, rain, land, time. They're all here—ready to be utilized.

God put them here for man's use and for man's benefit. Man doesn't own anything! God *owns it* . . . and loans it to man!

The Bible takes this very seriously. So much so in fact that it asks the question, "Will a man rob God!" God Himself asks the question!

That man is robbing God who refuses to put God first in the matter of possessions. "Giving to God is not a matter of generosity! It is a matter of honesty . . . of spiritual integrity!

The Christian man is admonished to give systematically. And the only Bible standard for systematic giving is the tithe, the first tenth of what a man makes. This belongs to God . . . after that, a man gives offerings.

No man has ever been the loser in putting God first. God

will be no man's debtor. But He expects a man to learn to put Him first—for the man's sake, not God's.

"Give, and it will be given to you; good measure, pressed down, shaken together, running over . . . " (Luke 6:38).

Invincible Men

"All the water in the ocean cannot sink a ship—unless the water starts getting inside. . . ."

"All the troubles in the world can't sink a human being . . . unless those troubles invade his inner life"—Vera Werblo, *Prairie Farmer*.

Strength inwardly is what counts in the long pull! Not how strong a man seems to be outwardly, but the resilience, the bounce-back, the inner tenacity—is what produces in life.

There's a vast difference between toughness and hardness! Some men are just hard, inflexible, unyielding. They won't ever give. But when pressure gets too heavy, they break! No inner strength—they cave in—collapse!

Toughness in men comes from within. It comes with the development of inner resources. This is what makes a man a good finisher! And it's the finish that counts in the pay-off!

There are men who start with a blast—like a torpedo . . . but they fizzle out before the finish! They don't carry through to the target. Their energy's spent—when it's most needed!

Other men start slowly, but they endure! They get hit, but they bounce back. Troubles converge—seem destined to wreck them—but they plow right through! They may lose battles, but they win the war!

Nothing stops them because they have inner resources that respond offensively every time things get rugged and rocky.

The surest way to build these inner resources is a steady, consistent use of the Bible daily: reading, studying it, memorizing it! This combined with regularity in prayer will make a man unbeatable!

Bible-believing, God-fearing men have been the backbone of America. Only one thing can whip America and that is forgetting God, neglecting the Bible. You've simply got to take time for the Bible and prayer daily! It makes man and nation invulnerable! It guarantees maximum strength!

Time alone with God is absolutely imperative for the man who desires to be his best! It tempers, seasons, settles the man . . . builds strength into the very fiber of his life!

"They who wait for the LORD shall renew their strength . . . " (Isa. 40:31).

The Set Mind

"One ship sails east—another west—By the selfsame wind that blows. . . . It's not the gale—but the set of the sail . . . that determines which way they go."

The first time a man watches sailboats on a bay he is struck with this strange fact that boats can sail in opposite directions driven by the same wind.

One of the Bible's most practical lessons is illustrated by the law of the sail and the wind!

Some men are driven to distraction and despair by the wind of circumstance. Trouble comes—defeat—failure—tragedy . . . and they cave in or collapse under pressure.

Or temptation comes, and they go down—whipped. They don't seem to have any resistance to trials or temptations or testings. Every change of wind blows them in another direction . . . often in circles.

Other men go through the same circumstances and they are tempered—mellowed—seasoned—matured. Everything that happens to them—every trial and testing—every temptation builds them up into stronger sharper men.

The same wind blows in each life, but one is driven to destruction and the other is driven further along on his course—toward his goal!

The difference is *the set of the mind!*

The man who sets his mind on himself—his own pleasures or selfish ends—gets tied up in knots and comes apart at the seams under the stress and strain of difficulty and trial.

He takes failure or defeat or mistakes as final. Disappointment means frustration, chaos, despair. And often such a man blames God for his mistreatment. (Although he never thanks God when things go right!)

A man sets his mind on God! He believes in God and follows Him! He is not an escapist! He doesn't seek trouble morbidly, but he doesn't run from it either!

He takes everything that happens to him as an opportunity to learn—to grow—to develop into a stronger, wiser, better man. Tragedy is never final but it is a means, a part of the processing of life. Disappointment is his appointment!

He never blames God. He looks for the blessing of God in whatever happens to him. He lets all winds drive him—on course—toward his destination!

"To set the mind on the flesh is death, but to set the mind on the Spirit is life and peace. . . . In everything God works for good with those who love him, who are called according to his purpose" (Rom. 8:6, 28).

Key to Reality

A professional man came to the office one day deeply discouraged. He wanted an answer for spiritual depression.

His Christian life had turned sour on him. He'd lost his taste for spiritual things. He was going through the motions, but there was no meaning to them. Just form without content. In a miserable rut, he still believed, but there was no reality to his faith. Just duty!

Actually faith had deteriorated into mere belief in creed. And creed didn't seem important. Prayer wasn't real. He didn't get any "lift" from Sunday worship.

As we talked, it became increasingly clear that this man had missed the first point of keeping faith alive. He had neglected his daily time of fellowship with Christ in prayer and Bible reading.

Of course it had become unreal! You go long enough without seeing your closest friend—without any fellowship or intercourse—and he will become unreal to you. Naturally!

The reason things got stale for this man was simply that he was failing to spend time with the Lord Jesus Christ, and the reality of His presence faded. Inevitably faith became empty form—no substance.

There's nothing magical about the Christian life. Neglect the daily diet of spiritual food and you're bound to suffer. You can't neglect meals and still be strong. "Three squares" a day are essential for the average busy man.

And a man's inward strength comes only with nourishment! Our faith feeds on the Word of God. Neglect this daily diet and the soul suffers. The danger is that one can go much longer without being conscious of spiritual malnutrition.

This is the crucial point of discipline in the Christian life!

111

A man needs to guard at all cost this constant daily spiritual nourishment: prayer and Bible reading and meditation.

The stories are legion of big men—strong men—productive men—who kept this vigil with God daily: thirty minutes or more alone with Him every day. *This is the most important thing in a Christian man's life!*

It does not mean a man gets a thrill every time he opens the Bible. But it does mean that whether he's conscious of it or not—whether he enjoys it or not—whether he really understands all he reads or not, his soul will be fed! Man is built that way! Just as a baby grows on its mother's milk though in ignorance of its food value, so the Christian man grows when he feeds on God's Word regularly.

He's not conscious of growing, but when he obeys the laws of growth he does grow. The necessity of spiritual food cannot be overemphasized!

"Faith comes from what is heard, and what is heard comes by the preaching of Christ" (Rom. 10:17).

God-planned Life

"But I want to be able to see God's plan all the way through to the finish!" insisted the man.

Strange how a man can demand such an impossible thing of God—and be bitter about it. It is not impossible for God, but it is for man! It's utterly unreal to insist on being shown the whole way. It simply doesn't work out in real life!

Because man is not equipped to see the whole plan! A trip to Canada was all worked out on a road map. The maps were stretched out on a table. We saw the whole trip from Los Angeles to Canada and back.

But they didn't begin to tell the story of the trip! We had to travel those miles to experience them. Every turn in the road and the crest of every hill brought new delights—new thrills.

The maps couldn't possibly show us these things or give us these thrills. Nor could they tell of the flat tires, the detours, the running out of gas, the trials we would have liked to escape.

(Strangely enough, the troubles helped to make the trip more enjoyable! Not when they were happening! But now that it's over, we talk much about the trials and get some of our biggest laughs out of them!)

We saw the whole plan on the maps. But we really didn't see anything when you get right down to it! We had to take the trip: mile by mile—hour by hour—incident by incident—before it meant anything to us.

Suppose we could have gone high enough in a plane to see the whole plan? It would be only a blob and a blur. Nothing distinct—nothing real!

Something else too: What if a man could see the whole plan? He'd try to by-pass the troubles that conceal some of life's greatest blessings . . . and he'd be so preoccupied with the good things of the future—he'd miss what was right under his nose.

Furthermore, actually seeing the whole plan laid out from beginning to end would not inspire confidence! It would not be real. It would be like a picture or a map.

What does inspire confidence is the knowledge that God is leading every step of the way. Every single moment is in His control! Providing a man wants it that way and yields to God's will. This is the assurance a man needs! This is the assurance we have!

When a man stops whining for the whole plan, and takes

life as it comes, realizing he can count on God every moment and every step, he begins to live as the Christian man should. He has a life of confidence and strength.

This is real freedom—real efficiency—real productivity. The man who walks with God is ready for anything! God wants you to walk with Him. He's ready . . . whenever you're ready to start!

"The LORD knows the way of the righteous, but the way of the wicked will perish . . ." (Ps. 1:6).

Authentic Freedom

When is a man really free? What constitutes freedom—true freedom among men?

At first thought the average man would probably say: "I'm free!" But is he? Are men really as free as they like to think?

Free politically and economically and socially. Free to worship God as he pleases. Free to speak his mind—to think his way—to make a living—to pursue happiness. But is that all there is to freedom?

Here's a man who'd swear he's free. But he's selfish! He's not free not to be selfish! He doesn't want to be this way; he criticizes selfishness in others, yet he's constantly embarrassed by selfishness in himself. Much as he hates it, he's in bondage to self. He's not really free!

Another man is not free not to lust! He's ashamed of lust in his life. He fights it with all his power. But again and again lust burns in his heart. He won't admit it—either to himself or others—but it's there. He resists it, but it has an iron grip. He's not really free!

Or there's the man who's not free from pride. He admires humility in other men, and thinks of humility as the supreme virtue. Yet time and again he's humiliated by things he's said and done that pride provoked. Pride dominates his life, causing burning shame and regret. He despises it, but he's bound by it. He's a long way from being a free man!

Take the man with an ungovernable temper. Who can measure the wounded hearts, the lost causes, the broken dreams, the wrecked lives that his uncontrollable anger causes? Is a man free when he's a slave to his temper?

Men otherwise strong and wise are pitifully and tragically bound by inner emotions and damnable dispositions that rule and reign in their hearts dictating words and deeds and attitudes that they despise!

Like Alexander the Great who wept because there were no more worlds to conquer, and cursed himself for his own lack of self-control. He conquered the world—and was pathetically defeated by himself!

The list is almost endless of the tyrants that rule in men's hearts. Tyrants that devastate lives and homes and businesses. Tyrants that shackle and bind strong men, making them helpless slaves: jealousy, covetousness, envy, greed.

This is precisely why Jesus Christ is the only adequate Savior! He frees a man inwardly and breaks the shackles of an evil disposition. When Christ rules in a man's heart, He emancipates that man completely!

"I am crucified with Christ—nevertheless I live—yet not I—but Christ liveth in me. . . ." "The law of the spirit of life in Christ Jesus hath set me free from the law of sin and death" (Apostle Paul).

Ask Christ to free you. He will!

By Faith

There's nothing complicated about faith when it is rightly understood. Or put another way, there's something wrong with the faith that is complex and difficult.

Actually faith is a simple thing—constantly and continually active in the life of a man. He acts on faith in his daily life again and again without ever giving it a thought.

He eats in restaurants thereby putting implicit faith in the chef that the food served him will not poison him. He sits in chairs implicitly believing they will support his weight.

He'll consummate transactions involving faith at almost every turn. In fact, the man who refused to live by faith would be so involved in putting to the test daily experiences that progress would be literally impossible.

Here's an example. A business deal is closed and sealed with a check. Now a check is nothing more than a man's promise to pay. The check is only as good as the drawer.

The payee takes the check in good faith, believing in the integrity of the maker. The time comes when the man needs to use the check. Without a qualm he turns it over—endorses it—uses it like cash. The whole deal is one of faith.

If the maker of the check has non-sufficient funds, or if the check is fraudulently drawn, all the faith in the world will not keep it from bouncing. It's not the faith of the payee, but the integrity of the maker that counts.

The same is true in a man's relation to God. The Bible abounds in the promises of God. The writers of Scripture insist that God's promises are immutable—or unchangeable. *When God says something it stands!*

Christian faith simply rests in the integrity of God. It takes

God at His word and acts on it. As the man endorses the check when he needs funds, so the Christian acts on God's promises in time of need.

Because God's promises are true, they work. They will not work if a man will not act on them by faith, any more than a check will work if a man refuses to endorse it. Endorsement is an act of faith.

The Christian has learned to rely on God's word. He takes a promise, acts on it, and lives as though it were true. And it works—because it is true. This is the most practical way of life—the only way of life in fact.

If God cannot be trusted, if He cannot be taken at His word, who then can! This makes sense! Learn to take God at His word. Believe what God says. Act on it. You'll find it works every time. God never fails!

"Commit your way to the LORD; trust in him, and he will act" (Ps. 37:5).

Use Trouble and Grow

It's not what happens to a man, but what he does after it happens that really counts in his life. You may not be able to stop people from kicking you, but you can determine the direction you go when they kick!

It's not the man who avoids or endures difficulty, but it's the man who uses difficulty who comes out right in the pay-off. Not what happens—but how you take it! That's the ticket!

No man is immune to trouble! Difficulty, failure, and tragedy happen to everyone. They are part of life—part of the process of living and growing! These things make or break a man depending on how he takes them!

Some men get the idea that to live is to escape difficulty. What they fail to realize is that difficulty is the means whereby a man is built up—strengthened—sharpened. Trouble tempers and seasons the man!

Imagine a golfer insisting all the difficulties be removed from the course: level all the bunkers; fill and returf the sand traps; straighten out the dog legs; fill in the water holes; eliminate the out-of-bounds. What kind of a course would that be? Who'd want to play it?

Those bunkers and sand traps are not there to hinder a man's game! They're to help it! The easy course is not the interesting one. There's no challenge to it. The good golfer goes a long way to find a tough course!

You can take difficulty or tragedy or failure as a problem! Or you can take them as possibilities! Every adverse thing that happens can become an opportunity to grow . . . a stepping stone, not a stumbling block!

Some men need the whine knocked out of them. They fold under the slightest handicap. Usually they blame everyone else for their trouble, and miss the blessing that trouble brings.

Character cannot be imputed . . . it must be developed, like muscle! The difficulties of life will develop character, if a man will face them and use them. Rivers get crooked dodging difficulties. So do men!

Here's the whole point of the Christian life. Christ not only helps a man live forever, He helps a man live now! Eternal life is a kind of life as well as everlasting. It begins when a man begins following Christ.

"Jesus Christ took the worst thing that could happen to Him—the cross . . . and turned it into the best thing that could happen—redemption!" He does that for every man who submits to Him and follows Him. Christ does not change the man's circumstances—He changes the man and makes him master of his circumstances!

"Do not pray for easy lives," says Phillip Brooks, "pray to be stronger men! Do not pray for tasks equal to your powers; pray for powers equal to your tasks!"

"My grace is sufficient for you . . ." (2 Cor. 12:9).

Big Men Are Thankful

You don't have to spend much time in the Bible to be conscious of the importance that is given to thankfulness! Thanksgiving is one of the most important attitudes a man can have. "In everything give thanks. . . ."

There is a reason why thanksgiving is so important! The absence of it indicates a fundamental deficiency in a man's character! Thanklessness is characteristic of little men with small souls and shallow lives.

In fact, thanklessness is one of the clearest symptoms of a sinful nature in man. "Although they knew God, they did not honor God or give thanks to him, but they became futile in their thinking and their senseless minds were darkened. Claiming him to be wise, they became fools."

This statement from the Epistle to the Romans (1:21–22) is part of the *divine diagnosis* of the human problem. At bottom, the thankless man is a sinful man, because he is godless in his attitude and practice.

This is sin in its essence—at its root. This is the disease in the heart of man from which springs the corruption that breeds discontent, greed, lust, war. Another word for it is secularism . . . or materialism!

The thankless man lives and acts as though God were not real at all! As though God were just an idea—good perhaps—but impractical, unreal, irrelevant. Though he says he believes in God . . . he acts as if he doesn't! Theistic in theory, he is atheistic in practice.

Such a man gives himself all the credit. He takes all the good things in life as though they belong to him by virtue of his own effort and ability. When you see thanklessness from this side, you recognize it as arrogance—pride—indifference to God. The thankless man professes to be "self-made!"

He forgets or ignores the fundamental teaching of the Bible that God is the owner of all things, and that man is simply a steward of these things. They belong to God . . . He loans them to man to use, to produce, to live by! This kind of man becomes his own little god. Ego is his idol!

It goes without saying that the thankless man is a little man, no matter how big he may seem to himself. The large-souled man is thankful because He is humble, recognizing how much of the good stuff of life he has by God's grace and mercy.

Try waking up each morning with some expression of thanksgiving—even when you don't feel like it. Let your first thoughts be toward God in gratitude for another day with opportunities.

Thank God through the day for the hundred-and-one things you usually take for granted: three square meals, a roof over your head, a job, friends, a wife and children, work to do, breath, beauty, strength, etc.

"Offer a sacrifice of thanksgiving . . ." (Amos 4:5).

Life's Transiency

Here's some information that was released several years ago. It is a most thought-provoking bit of observation. Think it through yourself.

In 1923 a group of the world's most successful financiers met at the Edgewater Beach Hotel in Chicago. Present were: the president of the largest independent steel company; the greatest wheat speculator; the president of the New York Stock Exchange; a member of the President's Cabinet; the greatest "bear" on Wall Street; the president of the Bank of International Settlements; the head of the world's greatest monopoly.

Collectively these tycoons controlled more wealth than there was in the United States Treasury . . . and for years newspapers and magazines had been printing their success stories, urging youth to follow their examples.

Twenty-five years later . . . let's see what happened to these men!

The president of the largest independent steel company—Charles Schwab—lived on borrowed money the last five years of his life . . . and died broke!

The greatest wheat speculator—Arthur Cutten—died abroad . . . insolvent!

The president of the New York Stock Exchange—Richard Whitney—was recently released from Sing Sing Prison.

The member of the President's Cabinet—Albert Fall—was pardoned from prison so he could die at home.

The greatest "bear" on Wall Street—Jesse Livermore—committed suicide!

The president of the Bank of International Settlements—Leon Fraser—committed suicide!

The head of the world's greatest monopoly—Ivar Krueger—committed suicide!

"Come now, you who say, 'Today or tomorrow we will go into such and such a town and spend a year there and trade and get gain'; whereas you do not know about tomorrow. What is your life? For you are a mist that appears for a little time and then vanishes. Instead you ought to say, 'If the Lord wills, we shall live and we shall do this or that'" (James 4:13–15).

Criteria for Success

From time to time we need to be reminded of the standard for greatness that Jesus Christ laid down in the New Testament. In these hectic, critical, unpredictable days when greed, selfishness, and exploitation are so rampant, we need that perspective!

In the matter of greatness, as in most other matters, the standards of Jesus are the antithesis of the standards of men. Whereas men are often superficial in their judgments, Jesus was basic, realistic, sound.

By many human standards that man is great who is in the place of being served. The man who can summon, with a word, a battery of secretaries or personal servants or clerks, is the man who has arrived. How he got there—whether or not he earned the right—does not enter into the consideration.

In the New Testament, by the standards of Jesus Christ, greatness is measured in terms of service. The greatest man is the one who serves most, who gives himself for the sake of others, without regard to the benefit that may accrue to himself.

Stop to think this through and you'll realize how fundamental it really is. It is only by superficial standards that men judge greatness in terms of being served, rather than in terms of service!

By and large the man who gets anywhere—who really succeeds—is the man who gives himself, without reservation, to the job to be done. He does a thing because it needs doing, not in order to get credit for it!

How many men today think of a good job not in terms of what is accomplished, not whether or not it is constructive, but in terms of hours or wages or ease. A good job is one where pay is maximum, hours minimum, and labor minimum. Examine it for what it is—it's the "get-the-most-for-the-least" philosophy. It's destroying America!

Such men never get very far because they never think in terms of what they can give a job. They think only in terms of what the job will give them. Little men they are . . . and they take up very little space in life!

Of course there are men who have risen to places of importance by accident! Men who have never earned the right to success—who have fallen into a place of prestige in spite of themselves. But what is more tragic than a little man in a big place?

These little men in big places are the exception, not the rule. Truly big men have earned the right to their place. In fact, in most cases they have made their place. They have done it by dint of service, by giving themselves to a job without regard for reward . . . without too much concern as to what they will get out of it! This is greatness!

Greatness in men is a number-one priority in America today. Little men in big places is one of our big problems. God help you to see the importance of service, of giving yourself unconditionally to the thing that needs to be done—for the sake of doing it!

"And whosoever would be first among you must be your slave . . ." (Matt. 20:27).

Evangelism—Every Man's Job

How seriously have you taken the New Testament teaching concerning the place of the Christian layman in the kingdom of God enterprise?

Rightly understood, the church of Jesus Christ is a lay movement! She really fulfills her function only when her laymen are active and operative. The church that gets top heavy with clergy control, bogs down, becomes static and often apostate.

The idea that evangelism belongs to a limited number of "professionals" who are pastors—or evangelists—is a caricature.

This kind of organization never lay in the mind of Christ. It was not the pattern followed at the inception of the church . . . nor was it held by the apostles.

Peter, for example, calls every believer in Christ a "priest." Every Christian has the right to come to God—without the mediation of an earthly priesthood. Paul addressed all Christians as "saints." All who are redeemed by Christ are saints according to the New Testament.

When Jesus began His public ministry, He did not commission raw recruits: young men—uncommitted to vocation or profession. On the contrary, He began with mature men who were settled—already committed to a vocation—men for whom life had pretty much jelled—laymen already active in secular pursuits.

There were 120 laymen gathered in the Upper Room on the day of Pentecost. Upon these the Holy Spirit fell—and the church was born. Those 120 laymen witnessed to the resurrection of Jesus Christ. They evangelized!

And 3000 responded to their witness and were baptized. These were men from "every nation under heaven." They were laymen who went back to their own land and broadcast the gospel of Jesus Christ. They evangelized!

When persecution set in at Jerusalem, the laymen were scattered abroad, and every place they went they witnessed. The apostles—the only ones who might be classified as "professionals"—remained at Jerusalem.

The first two effective evangelists, Phillip and Stephen, were laymen. The New Testament pages are full of the names of laymen—and women—who were the really active force in evangelism. That is the New Testament pattern!

Actually, you as a Christian man are indispensable to this program. God expects you to take part in the Christian witness. You have a little world you must reach for Christ—the world of your office, your home, your social circle! There is no escape from this obligation!

Communism has borrowed this program, and is exploiting it to the outside edge. *The church must match it* with laymen who dare to stand for Christ, and will propagate the gospel and infiltrate every area of life with a solid, vital, dynamic Christian witness. This is your task!

"Go ye into all the world—and preach the gospel to every creature."

Where Progress Begins

Suppose you decided to set out to change the world. Everyone agrees that changes are needed . . . things certainly are not as they ought to be!

If you really took this world mess seriously, and determined to do something about it—to throw your weight behind the changes that are needed—where would you begin?

Would you begin with the United Nations? That would seem at first thought the logical place. There is a key to the world situation, but would you be allowed a hearing . . . and if you were, what changes would you suggest?

Would you suggest a new system . . . a new kind of federation of nations . . . a new world government? You know instinctively that is not the answer.

Perhaps one ought to begin in Washington! Sometimes one would think that a change in Washington is going to wipe out the whole world mess in a brief time. But any thoughtful man knows that is impossible!

Besides, what sort of a change would you make in Washington? Fire some bureaucrats—some hangers-on—some political opportunist? That would help of course, but would it work any really basic change? Washington is smaller than the U.N., but it's still a complicated situation.

Maybe you should begin in your own community. Get next to the mayor, the council, the city manager. Suppose you could, what would you say? What would you do? What changes, really fundamental changes, would you make by changing your city government? Even that is complex and would not yield too easily to your pressure!

Well, how about your neighbors? Try to make them what they ought to be! You immediately realize how presumptuous that is! They wouldn't take to your changes too readily—if at all! You might create more problems than you'd eliminate.

When you take a moment to think it through, you realize that the basic problem, the fundamental need, is not in systems: international, national, or local government. Nor is it in industrial and business systems. The fundamental need is in the human heart—greed, selfishness, pride.

And where would one begin to change that? With himself of course! That's the place any important change must begin. Become yourself what you ought to be—what others ought to be if they were like you.

Suppose everyone were like you, what kind of a world would it be? What do you think would happen if every man who is really interested in seeing a better world would begin with himself? You know the answer! The world would change!

That's why Jesus Christ is the only adequate solution. He changes men! He makes them over—gives them a new nature. There is only one way to change inwardly, and that is to let Christ into your life—turn the controls over to Him.

"I am not ashamed of the gospel: it is the power of God for salvation to every one who has faith . . ." (Rom. 1:16).

Test for Truth

Nothing is more definite and explicit in the Bible than the fact that to Jesus Christ belongs the highest in the universe.

To all the Bible writers, and to Jesus Christ Himself, it was clear that He was infinitely more than a perfect man—more than a great teacher.

In fact, the Bible insists that Jesus Christ is the test for truth. What a man believes—or teaches—about Jesus Christ is the index to the truth of that man's belief, or teaching. A low view of Jesus Christ indicates error, or falsehood.

Take, for example, this clear statement in 1 John 4:1–3; ". . . do not believe every spirit, but test the spirits to see whether they are of God; for many false prophets have gone out into the world. By this you know the Spirit of God: every spirit which confesses that Jesus Christ has come in the flesh is of God, and every spirit which does not confess Jesus is not of God. . . ."

Now if Jesus Christ is nothing but mere man, perfect though He be, why should belief in His coming in the flesh constitute a test for truth? Why not any other great man, or great teacher, or religious leader?

The phrase "Jesus Christ . . . come in the flesh" signifies some very definite things. It means He existed before coming in the flesh. Which the Bible of course teaches (see John 1:1–2). It signifies that Jesus Christ—that One who actually lived in history—at a certain time, in a certain place—whose life divides history into B.C. and A.D., was actually, literally God come in human flesh!

Jesus Christ Himself knew this to be true. "Before Abraham was I am," He said to certain of His antagonists. "He who has seen me has seen the Father," He said to His disciples.

In the light of the clear teaching of Scripture it is difficult to understand the aversion in the hearts of many intelligent men to concede the highest place to Jesus Christ. They are willing to accept Him as a great man—a great teacher . . . one of the greatest . . . but they reject Him as unique!

It is important that you believe correctly about Jesus Christ, because to believe wrongly is not only to reject Him, it is to reject God, and truth itself. Christ is the one imperative issue in every man's life.

Obviously if a man believes wrongly about Jesus Christ, He will not turn to Him for salvation. But there is salvation in no other. He Himself—by His death on the cross—purchased eternal salvation for all who would believe.

A man must go this far at least—to confess his need and sin, to realize Christ died for Him on the cross, to receive His forgiveness.

"There is salvation in no one else . . . for there is no other name under heaven given among men by which we must be saved" (Acts 4:12).

"Stream of Humanity"

You have often heard human nature referred to as a stream— the "stream of humanity." Have you ever considered how really like a stream it is?

As the stream has its source in the highlands—the virgin, snow-clad peaks—so human nature had its beginning with God. Man was the peak of God's perfected creation. After everything else He made man, in His own image, for fellowship with Himself.

But the stream leaves its source, so man has turned from

God . . . left God out of his life, and lived as though God didn't matter.

The stream flows downhill—seeking irresistibly the lowest levels . . . never stopping, over and around, under and across, restlessly—impatiently—sometimes laughingly it flows—lower and lower . . .

Human nature too, seeks its lowest level . . . down—down—down to moral decay and spiritual ruin. But some will point to the progress, the advancement humanity has made. True! But only along technological lines, not morally or spiritually!

As the stream moves down the incline, it is constantly picking up dirt, debris, spoilage, carrying it along—adding to its corruption . . . except . . .

Here and there in its path are rocks. They will not move with the stream, will not loosen and float downhill, will not yield to the irresistible descent! These rocks purify the stream every few rods.

There are rocks in human nature! Men who refuse to budge, who are immovable! Christian men who are solid, clean, courageous. They will not yield to the descent and will not compromise. These men purify the life about them in the home, the office, the plant, in society.

Two kinds of men! Those who yield to the pull downward, who gravitate to the lower levels, and become part of the corrupting influence. Those who refuse to yield, who stand against the tide, who keep humanity from rotting altogether! To which group of men do you belong?

Finally, the stream finds its way to the ocean, dumps into it, and is lost in its abysmal depths . . . unless—and until—the sun lifts it back again into the heavens.

Human nature too, ends in the abyss . . . unless it allows itself to be lifted by the Son of God who laid down His life on the cross to redeem it. When a man yields to the pull of the Son, he is lifted back into fellowship with God!

One of the great historians of our day says the history of civilization can be told in one phrase of the New Testament: "The wages of sin is death. . . ."

"The wages of sin is death, but the free gift of God is eternal life . . ." (Rom. 6:23).

God Will Lead You

"If I could only know God's plan for my life!" said a friend in quiet desperation. "How can a man know what God's plan is?"

He was at the crossroads: still young, but not young enough to keep changing from one business to another. It was time he was settling down. He'd been successful at everything, but was dogged by a restlessness, a feeling he was not where he belonged.

If God really had a place for him, he wanted to know so he could "get with it." But he was pestered by the question, How does a man know?

Well, there's an answer! God does not tease men in this matter. He has given a clear, simple, workable answer. And when a man gets it, he's led to inward peace, top efficiency, and maximum productivity.

The Bible makes it quite explicit that God has a plan for every man! Jesus Christ spoke of this in a hundred different ways. It was the theme of the apostles and the Old Testament prophets.

But God does not—will not—force His will on a man. God does not coerce and does not impose His plan. *A man is free to yield or reject.* There is nothing "fatalistic" or inescapable about God's will.

This, however, is absolutely certain! Any man who wants God's best, who seeks God's will—can count on divine direction. Nothing delights God more than to lead men in His way.

The question is, How does a man know what God's plan is?

If by this a man means he wants to know all the details for the next fifty years, if it means he wants to see the road ahead to the end—around all the turns—over all the hills—through all the valleys, he's going to be disappointed.

Because this is not the way God's will works, as though it were a cut and dried thing like a blueprint or like a mold that had been cast. God's will is active—dynamic—immediate . . . like a potter shaping clay in his hands. It's a minute-by-minute—step-by-step affair!

What God does make absolutely clear is that He is leading: moment by moment—step by step. He establishes our thoughts, orders our steps, directs our paths.

We may not know the way God leads . . . but we know God leads! That's all that is important. He is absolutely trustworthy. He has promised to guide. His word is His bond! He can be depended upon—implicitly! We do not know the way, but we know the guide!

This is God's plan for every man—for you: Commit your life to Him. Surrender to His will daily. Ratify that surrender as often as necessary. Yield to His will—He does the leading. He guarantees it!

"Commit thy way to the LORD; trust in him, and he will act" (Ps. 37:5).

Strange Ideas of God

It would be amusing if it were not so pathetic—the ideas people get about God. Coming out of three weeks of Bible conference, with much personal consultation involved, one is especially aware of this.

One impression that has riveted itself to my mind is the feeling so many men have that they must overcome God's reluctance in one way or another before they can expect God to bless their lives.

It is as though God were unwilling to help a man, unless he met some very harsh and difficult conditions, or really earned the blessing, or in some way deserved God's attention.

Strange as it may seem, many men have this concept of God! They've got to work hard, struggle, strive in some indefinable way to placate God's anger or to earn God's favor.

Apparently in their mind, God sits—wherever God sits— with arms folded, a wry grin on His face, just daring anybody to ask Him for anything; and when they do, making the conditions so difficult it is next to impossible!

That's not the God of the Bible! The God of the Bible is the opposite of that.

If there is one thing the Bible teaches throughout, it is this—the reluctance is on man's part—not God's! The real problem in the God-man relationship is that man is not willing to let God help him.

God loves us with an everlasting love. He demonstrated

133

that love, proved it beyond the shadow of a doubt, by the crucifixion. God's love is unquenchable!

The cross is the symbol of His love. God is more anxious to bless us then we are to be blessed . . . more anxious to give us wisdom—strength—peace—than we are to take them. We are the ones who are reluctant—not God!

In fact, the definition of grace reveals this. "Grace is unmerited favor." Grace means we don't deserve it or are unworthy of it. If we deserve it, if we earn it, if we merit it, it is not grace! Grace means that in spite of our unworthiness, God loves us and wants to help us.

God is constantly, quietly, lovingly waiting for us to give in, to yield to Him, to consent to His lordship in our lives. He blesses—when we let Him!

There's only one condition a man must meet to receive God's choicest blessings! Man must admit his need, consent to God's help, and draw on God's resources!

And the only thing in the world that keeps a man from doing this is pride! That's why pride is the root sin, the arch-enemy of man. It keeps him from doing the sensible thing—the right thing—the best thing!

"My grace is sufficient for thee, for my power is made perfect in weakness" (2 Cor. 12:9).

Honest Doubt

Thomas couldn't swallow the Resurrection!

He was as close to Jesus as the other disciples. He heard the same words, saw the same miracles, watched the matchless

personality as He walked the dusty roads of Galilee, and stud-
ied the perfection of His life.

Thomas certainly heard Jesus when He said He was going to
rise from the dead, that the grave would not be the end, but it
didn't sink in.

So when the other disciples reported that Jesus had appeared to them three days after His crucifixion, Thomas
thought they were suffering an illusion, that the death of their
beloved Master had left them in shock.

Thomas shrugged off the report with these words: "Unless I
see in his hands the print of the nails, and place my finger in
the mark of the nails, and place my hand in his side, I will not
believe" (John 20:25).

Eight days later they were together again and Thomas was
with them. Jesus appeared and after a general greeting He
addressed Thomas: "Put your finger here, and see my hands;
and put out your hand, and place it in my side; do not be
faithless, but believing" (John 20:27).

Thomas didn't need to run a test on the Lord. He cried,
"My Lord and my God!"

Two things are significant. First, the personal interest Jesus
took in the incredulity of Thomas. Whenever a man has
difficulty with honest doubt, Jesus is the first to be willing to
resolve the doubt and dispel the difficulty.

Christianity is the religion of a "sound mind." Disciples of
Jesus do not have to scuttle their intellects and stop thinking.
Christian faith will bear the most probing, penetrating inves-
tigation!

It's not the doubter Jesus is unable to help, it's the man who
is unwilling to believe regardless of evidence. He is without
faith, not because he *can't* believe, but because he *won't* believe! This is unbelief in its raw form; refusal of evidence.

It's a problem of a man's will, not his intellect. When a man has intellectual problems with faith, Jesus will take a personal interest in solving them and at the same time allow the man to maintain his intellectual self-respect!

The second lesson in Thomas' experience is overwhelming! Apparently, Jesus bore the marks of crucifixion in His resurrection body. They were there when He spoke to Thomas. They are there today! They'll always be there!

The only One to bear the scars of sin in eternity will be the Son of God Himself! He who was the sinless One will be the sole reminder of the consummate consequences of sin. We who were sinners and redeemed will never be able to forget the price He paid!

What a paradox: the sinner forever free from the slightest trace of sin . . . the sinless Son of God bearing forever in His body the marks of sin's sacrifice.

How long has it been since you thanked Christ for dying for you?

God's Will

There's nothing mysterious about the will of God. It's like taking a trip. Following God's way is an exciting adventure. Life is never so interesting as when one takes the will of God seriously and walks in it!

Beginning a trip a man is sure of his destination, but he is not familiar with every mile of the way. That would turn a trip into boredom!

He usually has a map that points the way he should take—suggests some of the things he should see enroute.

As the traveler journeys, he sees as far ahead as the road permits. Sometimes many miles—sometimes but a few yards. A turn in the road, a hill, a clump of trees, any number of things may limit his view ahead.

But he doesn't get alarmed because he cannot see beyond the next curve or over the brow of the next hill. He knows that when he goes as far as he can see ahead, a new view waits to be unfolded before him.

Two things are imperative: First, he keeps on going even though he doesn't see very far ahead. Secondly, he sticks to the road. It was built to bring him to his destination. Obviously, it cannot if he refuses to take it!

This is life in the will of God! The destination is absolutely certain! Familiarity with every step of the way is unimportant! The Bible is the infallible map and guide. Jesus Christ is the road . . . the way!

The important thing is for a man to get on the road—and keep going!

It is as foolish to get nervous and anxious when God does not reveal all the way ahead as it would be to become distracted simply because one cannot see the highway over the hill or around the corner.

Imagine the traveler refusing to go forward until he could see the entire journey laid out before him. That would be the end of progress!

Walking in the will of God as far as one can see—no matter how brief the view—will lead inevitably to new vistas, new heights, new beauty! Doing the thing at hand is the surest guarantee there will be more to do!

Something more to be said: The traveler keeps his destination in mind. This helps over the rough spots. And there will be rough spots. Sometimes there are detours. Often these detours lead to the most fascinating experiences of the trip. Sometimes the traveler talks and laughs most about these when the trip is over. In retrospect they afford him the greatest joy.

Disappointments in life often prove to be His appointments. The detours unexpected and unexplained, do more for a man than anything else!

Keep your eye on Christ. Follow Him. And walk by faith! It's better than sight! It's the life of adventure and joy—and accomplishment!

Escapism Solves Nothing!

Suicide is the ultimate in the "geographic cure."

It doesn't "end it all," it only changes a man's location! Nothing is settled by it! After that comes judgment!

But it is a perfect illustration of the futility of escapism. A man never solves a problem by running away from it. He only aggravates and complicates it.

Escapism—or the geographic cure—takes many forms. A man may simply "drown his troubles in drink." He may get busy, so busy he forgets them. He may ignore his troubles up to a point, and act as though they do not exist . . .

Modern society has taught us many ways to live with our problems, but it has not told us how to solve them.

Modern methods of handling trouble appeal to the cowardice in man and encourage him to escape from reality, either by making himself pleasantly insensitive with a few social drinks, or by indulging in overeating and gluttony, or by more drastic means.

Many of the purported solutions work on the symptoms rather than the problem itself. They anesthetize a man against awareness, rather than help him root out the trouble and settle it once for all.

This is where genuine Christianity plays the strategic hand. It aims at the problem itself, not the symptoms; it provides a cure, not just a sedative.

The Christian way is to face the difficulty, admit it, then commit it to God!

Committing the matter to God does not absolve the Christian from responsibility. On the contrary, it equips him to handle it, gears him into the thing, so it becomes redemptive in his life, a stepping stone instead of a stumbling block.

The man who acknowledges his weakness and turns to God for help is not then turned into a weakling. He is in fact made strong—in the strength of God.

The most dependable man is the one who lives in dependence on God. The most self-reliant man is the one who has learned to rely on God.

Nowhere does the Bible promise the Christian smooth sailing, but God does guarantee a dependable charter for the course and arrival at the destination in excellent condition!

Nothing can "separate us from the love of God . . . in all these things we are more than conquerors through him who loved us . . ." (Rom. 8:39, 37).

The Devil You Say!

Do you believe in the devil? Nothing displeases his infernal majesty more!

He is the first to promote a man's disbelief. He deliberately arranges the evidence to prove his nonexistence. This is his tactical masterpiece: He convinces people that he isn't. "Satan's triumph is his incognito."

"Hell is a conspiracy. Like all good conspiracies, its first requirement is that nobody shall believe in it" (*Life* editorial, 2/2/48).

No intelligent person is afraid of "nothing." How better to put man off guard than to persuade him that belief in a personal devil is an illusion—a fraud—an infantile concept?

Satan does not like to be laughed at (no insincere person can bear this and he is the quintessence of insincerity) but he will endure even ridicule to distract men from belief in himself. Much as it injures the pride of this utterly egotistical one, he will submit to it to keep men from taking him seriously.

Satan is the prince of subversives! He is the supreme artist of deception and masquerade, the genius of camouflage.

He is the absolute opposite of God! He is good in reverse! He has transvalued all values, prostituted all virtue, perverted all motives, caricatured all beauty.

Evil is his good. Expediency is his principle. Indifference is his concern. Nonsense is his reason. Error is his truth. Anarchy is his law. Tyranny is his freedom. Lust is his love. Pride is his humility. Panic is his peace. Chaos is his order. Perversion is his virtue.

He is the arch conspirator for the allegiance of man, yet he tries never to let man know it. He will turn a man's affection anywhere if it will alienate the man from Christ, for only then can the man be made a tool for satanic purposes.

Jesus Christ so loved man that He laid down His life on the cross to redeem man. Satan so loves himself that he will destroy all men to achieve supremacy and a throne.

No adequate understanding of history can be had without taking into account the fact that behind and around and through history, a personal, diabolical, satanic, spiritual force is bent on destroying all good and its author, Jesus Christ.

In fact, no man will understand himself and his own troubles until he realizes that evil is more than mere absence of good . . . that evil is dynamic and personal, working to possess man's mind and heart, to coerce man to reject God's love and rule.

"For we are not contending against flesh and blood, but against the principalities, against the powers, against the world rulers of this present darkness, against the spiritual hosts of wickedness in the heavenly places" (Eph. 6:12).

The Word of a Gentleman

You may choose to be whipped by circumstances or triumphant in them, depending on whether you choose to believe the circumstances or the promises of God!

"It is the word of a Gentleman of the most strict and sacred honor, so there's an end to it," declared David Livingstone, the great pioneer missionary to Africa, in explaining his confidence in the promises of Jesus Christ.

Livingstone simply *took Jesus Christ at His word!* It was that simple. The promise of Christ as the promise of a Gentleman and that was the end of the matter!

This is the most down-to-earth application of Christian faith that can be made. The word of Jesus Christ can be depended upon implicitly. It is absolutely trustworthy! It can be taken at its face value.

Circumstances may be difficult, but this in no way alters the integrity of Christ nor the dependability of His promise.

At times a man will feel very much out of touch with God, when circumstances almost swamp him, but the word of God still stands. The man may change, or his circumstances, but *Christ is changeless!*

A man may fail, but Jesus Christ never! Man's failure does not mean His failure!

The wise Christian learns to count on the clear promises of God as they are laid down in the Bible. In times of stress and strain, pressure and tension, in times of personal defeat and failure, he turns to the promises and rests the full weight of his need there.

God's promises are utterly substantial! They will bear any weight a man may put on them. They stand up under any pressure. They are ageless—changeless—infallible!

The secret of a tranquil, efficient, triumphant life lies with the promises and their application to any and every issue of life.

Therefore, the first order of the day for the Christian is to familiarize himself with the promises. If he is not acquainted with them, they might as well not be there so far as he is concerned.

Which suggests why many a so-called Christian finds himself constantly defeated by circumstances. He is pathetically unaware of the uncounted promises of God stored up in the Bible like a rich deposit waiting for him to draw on whenever need arises.

Obviously a man can take no strength from a fact he does not know exists. So a man by neglecting the Bible remains ignorant of the promises that can carry him through any difficulty to victory.

He's a smart man who gets his nose in the Book every day to discover the wealth he has been given in Jesus Christ!

This Is Life

Being is more important than having!

It is possible for a man to have much and still be a pathetic failure, even in his own eyes!

Because what a man is, is infinitely more important than what a man has!

There are men who have acquired everything a man might seem to want in life, yet life has been empty and meaningless for them.

This is because God made man to be somebody, not just to have things!

Some of the most frustrated men in the world are those who seem to have everything. The more they have, the deeper their frustration.

This is really no mystery: life is being, not just having!

No intelligent man is satisfied with the respect of others, if that respect is based solely on what he possesses rather than on what he is.

In fact, this is the heart of the inexplicable loneliness of some "big men" who are never sure who their friends are. Secretly in their hearts they wonder whether they are recognized for themselves or for their possessions.

Would people love them, respect them as much without their possessions? Are they wanted because of the kind of men they are or because of what people hope to get out of them?

Some of the biggest men are the loneliest for this very reason!

Here is one of the glaring failures of our modern world: it has taught us how to get and have, but it has neglected to teach us how to be someone!

Science and technology have equipped us with the art of acquiring, but training in character has failed to keep pace. We are technical giants—moral and spiritual adolescents!

And the consummate product of our technology is a "Frankenstein" that may destroy us because we have been so preoccupied with possessing and so little concerned with what we are that we find ourselves spiritually unqualified to handle our knowledge of science.

This does not mean that God did not intend man to have things. But He did mean for man to use what he has for the glory of God! God meant man to possess his possessions, not to be possessed by them. Possessions were to be man's tool, not his master! Man was made to love people and use things . . . so often he loves things and uses people!

". . . a man's life does not consist in the abundance of his possessions" (Luke 12:15).

Supreme Fact!

What happened to the body?

According to the record, the body of Jesus Christ, which had been buried three days before, was missing . . .

His enemies would have paid any price to recover it. That would have settled the fact once and for all that the Resurrection was a fraud.

If they had been able to produce the corpse, Jesus Himself would have been completely discredited for He said He would rise from the dead . . . that His resurrection would validate all His claims and works.

But they couldn't locate the body. The best they could do was resort to a theory so utterly transparent that it is difficult to understand how any intelligent person could have taken it seriously.

". . . they gave large money to the soldiers, saying, 'Say ye, His disciples came by night and stole him away while we slept. . . .'" (If they were asleep how did they know what happened?)

Ever since that first insipidly weak attempt, men have tried in every generation to discredit the resurrection of Jesus Christ. Their theories have been equally ridiculous and have succeeded only in cancelling out themselves one by one.

Not one scrap of evidence has been offered in support of these theories! All the evidence supports the Resurrection! No fact of history is more thoroughly substantiated!

For six weeks following His resurrection, He walked on earth. He was seen often by disciples who themselves were most incredulous. It was difficult for them to believe that He was real. Thomas, for example, was very slow in accepting the fact.

The disciples were not deluded! They did not expect Him to rise! There has never been a more disillusioned, distraught, despairing group of people in history than Jesus' disciples following His crucifixion. His death blasted all their dreams.

Until they saw Him again! Saw Him—handled Him—heard Him over a period of forty days. Gradually through their bewilderment dawned the realization that He was alive!

It is utterly inconceivable that the disciples stole the body of Jesus—hid it—then boldly declared that He had risen, that they actually laid down their lives for it.

145

The body was not in the tomb because Jesus Christ had risen—actually! Literally! He is alive now! He is not a dead hero at whose tomb Christians worship. He is a living Lord—contemporary—close at hand—real!

Christians don't just believe in a creed. They know and trust and love a Person! He lived and died and rose again! The heart of Christian faith is allegiance to this Person. The power of Christian faith is His Presence within the body of the Christian!

"That which we have seen and heard we proclaim also to you, so that you may have fellowship with us; and our fellowship is with the Father and with his Son Jesus Christ" (1 John 1:3).

Redemption

A master violinist visits the pawnbroker.

He has fallen on evil days; his funds are low and reluctantly he finds it necessary to seek a loan.

With precious instrument in hand he calls at the shop with the three balls above the door. The pawnbroker appraises the violin and the transaction is made.

The master violinist leaves with the required funds—and a pawn ticket.

The pawnbroker places the violin on a shelf.

Two things are true of the violin as long as it is in the pawn shop. It is in the possession of one who is not its rightful owner, and it is not being used for the purpose for which it was created. It gathers dust on a shelf!

Better days come. The violinist is able to claim his precious instrument. He hurries to the pawn shop, presents ticket and money with interest. In return he is given his violin. He rushes home.

Breathlessly he enters his studio, opens the violin case, dusts off the valuable instrument, tightens and resins the bow, and begins to play the exquisite music the violin had been created to produce.

Now the violin belongs once more to its rightful owner. Now it is doing that for which it was made.

That is redemption!

It is the theme of the Bible, and it is precisely what Jesus Christ came into the world to do. Redemption is at the heart of Easter!

Man was in the possession of one who was not his rightful master—Satan. He was not being used to do that for which he was created . . . glorify God!

These two things are true of the unredeemed man! He may be a good man, an ethical man, cultured, refined . . . even religious, but he is in the possession of a usurper, and his life is being used for something less than was intended.

At the awful price of His own blood on the cross, Jesus Christ redeemed man. He came into the world as the "Lamb of God"—as a "sacrifice for sin."

Don't let yourself miss the point of Easter. Take Jesus Christ at face value. Accept Him on His terms—not on diluted human terms.

He was Teacher—yes. Example—yes. But first and foremost, Savior—Lamb of God! His teaching, His life, point to His cross. He was born to die!

By virtue of His willing sacrifice all men who trust in Him will live—forever! This is the stupendous significance of Easter! May it mean nothing less to any man.

"I am come that they might have life and have it more abundantly. . ."

Belief

Words have a way of degenerating through common usage . . .

So it is with the biblical word "believe."

Belief is infinitely more than simply accepting a creed—more than mere intellectual assent to dogma.

In the Bible, belief involves a Person!

Christian belief means trust in that Person plus surrender and commitment to Him. Anything less than personal trust and commitment falls far short of belief in the biblical sense.

Long before the disciples had developed doctrines about Jesus, long before they understood Him for that matter, they trusted Him and followed Him!

They could not understand Jesus Christ any more than His enemies could, but they followed Him, whereas His enemies tried to destroy Him.

The disciples knew very little about Christ . . . but they knew Him! The facts of His life were stubborn—incontrovertible. They could not explain Him, but they trusted Him. They "went along" with Him.

His enemies believed too, in the sense that they could not deny the facts. The facts were unmistakable—indisputable—and it was these facts they could not deny that made His enemies spare no effort to liquidate Him.

They would not accept Jesus, but they had to believe because He shattered every argument they raised against Him—blasted every theological attempt they made to discredit Him.

They believed, but they would not follow! They believed, but they would not be His disciples!

If they could have discredited Him they probably would never have had to crucify Him. But their arguments collapsed in the face of the facts and they had no recourse but to get rid of the One whose life bankrupted every effort to prove Him an imposter.

The disciples believed too. They faced the facts that were a matter of public record. (To this extent their belief was intellectual.) But more than this they trusted Him—surrendered their allegiance to Him. (In this respect their belief involved their wills.)

True belief is intelligent to the extent that a man accepts certain facts that are basic to Christian faith, but it is a great deal more: it is intensely personal. Having accepted the facts, the Christian gives his life to Christ, to walk in surrender and obedience.

That's why belief changes a man, because Christ has the power to change him. Belief implies commitment. Christ is the Lord of the Christian!

"Therefore, if any one is in Christ, he is a new creation; the old has passed away, behold, the new has come" (2 Cor. 5:17).

How to Give

How a man gives money is more important than how much he gives!

The spirit of giving, rather than the amount of the gift, is of primary importance in the true Christian view.

Three New Testament suggestions for giving will bless the

giver far beyond the measure of the gift and make giving a pleasant responsibility instead of an undesirable duty.

(1) Giving should be systematic: ". . . as God has prospered. . . ." Unplanned—indiscriminate—hit-and-run giving misses the point entirely. Careless giving is "care less" giving!

The first law of stewardship is that God has top priority in man's affairs; therefore, man should figure God in (so to speak) a business-like way. Setting aside a regular portion of his income for God is man's way of recognizing that all of life is a trust from God.

(In the Bible the only standard given is the tithe—the first tenth . . . this is the least a Christian should do.)

(2) Giving should be cheerful: ". . . not of necessity for God loves a cheerful giver." The man who gives reluctantly under pressure had far better not give! A gift wrongly given leaves acid in the soul and giving turns sour. Let the man who gives grudgingly keep his gift!

Man is absolutely free not to give! God guarantees this freedom and will not Himself violate it.

Furthermore God does not need man's money! He is not bankrupt! But man needs to give! Stewardship is God's highest favor bestowed only on man. The beasts of the field know nothing about this. The man who has not caught the secret of stewardship is less than a man!

Man gives, not because God needs the gift, but because man needs to share in the divine enterprise. This is life's highest order—man at his best: "Workers together with God."

In His grace God allows man the supreme prerogative: a stake in eternal business! Man is given the priceless privilege of investing in God's program. The dividends are guaranteed.

The interest is eternally compounded. The satisfaction is everlasting. What a deal!

(3) Giving should be "to the Lord." Though given through human institutions, it should be presented to God. "Give every gift," one has put it, "as though you were placing it into the nail-pierced hands of Jesus Christ Himself."

Give as to the Lord—not to men . . . to be seen of the Lord—not for the praise of man!

"Do not lay up for yourselves treasures on earth, where moth and rust consume and where thieves break in and steal, but lay up for yourselves treasures in heaven, where neither moth nor rust consumes and where thieves do not break in and steal . . ." (Matt. 6:19–20).

"Give, and it will be given to you; good measure, pressed down, shaken together, running over . . ." (Luke 6:38).

Seeing the Invisible

Can a man see what is invisible?

The Bible tells us this was the secret of Moses' ability to weather every storm of life. "He endured as seeing the invisible. . ."

This was the heart of Moses' greatness . . . it is the heart of greatness in any man!

The great artist is the one who can see the finished portrait before he begins to splash his oils against the canvas.

The great sculptor is the one who sees the thrilling statue in a crude block of rough marble.

The great architect is the one who can see the cathedral before the blueprints are drafted or the elevation has been drawn.

151

Behind every great movement—every great institution—every great achievement is a man who could see the invisible before it became a reality.

This was true of the Son of God who "for the joy that was set before him endured the cross, despising the shame. . . ."

He looked beyond the indescribable humiliation and suffering of Gethsemane and Calvary to the joy of men redeemed from the long-term consequences of their sin. He looked beyond the agony, to the glory of emancipated men.

He looked at Simon, the weak, vacillating, impetuous, blustering fisherman . . . and He saw Peter—the rock!

He looks into your life and sees you, not as you are with your failure and weakness and sin, but as He can make you . . . if you let Him rule in your heart and life.

It all depends on where a man looks: He can look at things as they are . . . or he can look at things as Jesus Christ is able to make them.

He can look at circumstances (outside himself or within himself) with all their implications and complications—their knots—their frustrations, and that is exactly what he will see: the circumstances . . . and be overwhelmed by them!

Or he can look to Jesus Christ who "holds the whole wide world in His hands." He can fill his mind and heart with Christ's promises, remind himself of God's presence and power. He can look beyond the circumstances to the absolute integrity of God—and be "more than a conqueror!"

He can look to himself—or to Christ; the choice is his. Each man decides where he is going to look: he chooses to trust circumstances or to trust Christ. He chooses to be victimized by the visible, or to be victorious seeing the invisible.

". . . let us run with perseverence the race that is set before us, looking to Jesus the pioneer and perfecter of our faith . . ." (Heb. 12:1–2).

What Is a Christian?

What is a Christian? Not what does he do, but what is he? He is a man in whose life God has worked the supreme miracle, the miracle of the new birth—spiritual regeneration.

A Christian is a twice-born man. Literally! Born first when he entered this world . . . born again when Christ entered his life.

Being twice-born he has two kinds of life: The life he received from his parents at his first birth, and the life received from God at his second birth. The first is human and temporal, the second is divine and eternal.

That is to say, the Christian has two distinct natures: the "old" nature—product of his first birth—and a new nature infused into him at second birth.

But birth is only a beginning. Growth follows as a normal process, providing the conditions for growth are met. This is true of the Christian's new (spiritual) nature as well as his "old" (human) nature. Both have requirements for growth.

A man eats, gets proper rest and exercise . . . and he grows! If he refuses food, neglects rest and exercise . . . his body suffers. Likewise the new nature requires nourishment and rest and exercise to be vigorous and healthy—to grow normally.

It is a tragedy when a child fails to grow physically and mentally. It is an infinitely greater tragedy when a Christian fails to grow spiritually! Adults who remain spiritual infants are just as serious a problem as are those who fail to grow in other areas.

The new nature feeds on the Word of God which is its milk and bread and meat. It is exercised by prayer, witnessing, and service. It "rests" in worship and fellowship. It takes all these—consistently followed—to produce a mature Christian.

And conversely, no matter how hard a Christian struggles to live "the good life," so-called—he falls miserably short of the healthy, vital, spiritual adult if he neglects the Word of God—the worship of God—fellowship—prayer and service.

An important observation: birth and growth are not conscious experiences. A man knows he was born, not because he remembers the experience, but because he is now alive. He knows he is growing, not because he feels it, but by comparing what he is with what he was.

The Christian knows he is "born again," not because he has had some sudden, emotional experience (though some do), but because he is spiritually alive now. Not because he can "hark" back to a moment when something happened to him (though some can), but because God is now personal and real to him, because he now trusts Christ as his Savior and Lord.

By the same token he knows he is growing spiritually, not because he feels the process taking place, but because of what he is compared to what he was.

"To all who received [Christ] . . . he gave power to become children of God" (John 1:12).

How to Begin

"How do you accept Christ?" the man asked impatiently.

He'd been in on a discussion in which the leader used the phrase loosely without an explanation. Impatience built up and exploded in the question, "How do you do it?"

It is simple—not complicated. It is like being introduced to a person, then cultivating the acquaintance. This is precisely the heart of Christianity: a personal relationship—a "living" contact between two people: a man and Christ!

Moreover, it is misleading to boil it down to a single formula, as though there is an "only" way to accept Christ. Actually, there are many ways when it comes to details. Each disciple responded differently to Christ: Peter and Andrew for example. Paul's conversion was distinct from John's. In a sense, each man comes his own way.

But while details differ, there is a basic essential involved that is identical: The important thing is the personal relationship, however it is expressed.

It is possible to know a lot about a person without knowing him. Abraham Lincoln, for instance, is familiar to us, but we never had the pleasure of knowing him. So men may know much about Christ, yet not really know Him. A man may acquire a knowledge of theology, and Christ may remain an utter stranger to him.

The point is, knowing anyone begins with a decision—a choice—an open heart. A man can refuse to meet or cultivate friendship with another man. Likewise, a man may ignore Christ insofar as a personal encounter with Him is concerned.

Take this data often used to "introduce" men to Christ and perform a personal experiment to your own satisfaction. Two propositions, two conditions . . . and a promised result.

"To all who received him [Christ] . . . he gave power to become children of God . . ." (John 1:12). The condition: receive Christ. The promised result: He will give you power to become a son of God. The question is, how does a man "receive Christ"?

"Behold, I stand at the door and knock; if any one hear my

voice and opens the door, I will come in to him" (Rev. 3:20). The condition: open the door. Promised result: Christ will enter.

Jesus says He will enter a man's life if that man will open the door. When He does enter, He gives that man power to become a son of God. The big question is, will the man open the door? The door to a man's heart is his will. Either he will or he won't!

Right now, as this selection is being read, you may prove for yourself the validity of Christ's promise. He is knocking. Will you receive Him? Will you allow Him to enter your life and make you a son of God? If so, tell Him. Invite Christ into your heart right now!

If you will, then according to His word He will enter. If you have, He has!

Conversion

"Except you be converted, you shall not enter into the kingdom of heaven."

Jesus Christ said that!

But what does it mean? What is it to be converted? Is it a complicated theological matter with little or no practical value or application?

On the contrary—as with other good words in the Bible, this word does not have some difficult, mysterious, theological implication that requires special interpretation or education.

Jesus spoke it to common men: men who were largely unschooled and unlearned—plain, simple men. He spoke in the vernacular, the language of the common man and not in the classical language of the scholar.

Jesus made sense to the man in the street. His words carried to Mr. Averageman. He touched life at the grass roots, right where people live.

And when He said "converted," it was understandable to those who heard. He intended it to be taken in its plain, unvarnished, simple meaning.

To convert electricity is to change current. Conversion means change!

Following World War II, factories were converted. They had been producing instruments of war—they re-tooled to produce for peace. The tank factory began turning out automobiles.

Ships were converted. They had been carrying troops to war, now they were made into luxury liners carrying passengers commercially.

Conversion means "re-tooling" for another purpose. It means put to new use.

The unconverted man needs "change" because he is being used for a purpose other than for what he was intended. He is being used the wrong way—going the wrong way.

In fact, this gives a hint to the basic idea of sin. "All we like sheep have gone astray; we have turned every one to his own way" (Isa. 53:6).

This is sin: To go one's own way, indifferent to God's will. It means to follow self instead of God, to serve one's own purpose rather than God's.

To convert is to decide for God. It means an about face, a new direction in life. It means to choose deliberately to go God's way.

157

The unconverted man cannot enter the kingdom of heaven—not because God prevents him, but because he prevents himself by his own choice! It is God's will that the man enter . . . but he chooses contrarily.

"Whosoever will may come," Jesus said. It's up to each man to choose. God has made the way through Jesus Christ. But He will not—cannot force a man.

"Except you choose . . . you shall not enter the kingdom of heaven."

Security

Christian faith is not a "hope-so" proposition.

Certainty is the hallmark of faith! Not rigid, inflexible, complacent, stuffy cocksureness—but certainty, assurance rooted in knowledge.

The Christian who is unsure or fearful or tentative in his faith is missing one of the genuine benefits that accrue to him.

In the New Testament the word "hope" is used as a noun—not a verb. Hope is not something a Christian does . . . it is something he has. It is a possession! It is not wishful thinking or castles in the air or "pie in the sky by and by!" It is the conviction of the inevitable and final triumph of Jesus Christ in history and beyond!

The Christian hope is sure and steadfast, and the Christian knows it cannot fail.

Christian faith is not hoping . . . it is knowing!

This does not mean absence of doubt. A thoughtful Christian may entertain doubts from time to time (the apostle

Thomas doubted, for example), but in the midst of the doubt there is a deep-down, fundamental sense of security.

Furthermore, Jesus Christ will satisfy the honest doubter with evidence that resolves doubt and establishes a man more firmly in faith. The only man who cannot be thus satisfied is the man who refuses to be. Even God is unable to help the man who rejects the evidence.

Christian hope is sure because it is grounded in the integrity of God. It cannot fail because God cannot fail.

Christian certainty rests on the absolute faithfulness of God: His unfailing, everlasting love—His irrevocable promise—His unswerving justice.

Christian certainty centers in Jesus Christ: the perfection of His life, the atoning power of His crucifixion, the eternal victory of His resurrection.

Back of Christian certainty is the word and work of Christ who said: "He who hears my word and believes in Him who sent me, has everlasting life and shall not come into condemnation because he is passed from death to life."

The Christian is sure, not because of himself: his ability to live up to something or keep on or hold out, but because Christ is sure! By His life and death and resurrection, Jesus Christ guarantees unequivocally eternal life to every man who trusts Him.

It is not conceit for a Christian to be certain of heaven. It is a reproach to Christ for him not to be. Uncertainty does not reflect against the Christian . . . it reflects against Christ.

The man who is safe from the eternal consequences of his sin, who is sure of everlasting life, is not counting on his own merit or ability . . . he is counting on the merits of the redemptive work of Christ.

"Not because of deeds done by us of righteousness, but in virtue of his own mercy he saved us" (Titus 3:5).

Good . . . for What?

Take God out of good—what do you have left? You have "O" left—exactly nothing. There's a lesson in that!

There's much more to life than just being good. Plenty of people are good—like a statue. They never make a mistake—never make anything else either. They never do anything wrong—don't do anything else! It's not enough to be good. One must be good for something.

Examine the goodness of the average man today. What are his reasons for being good? He's afraid he'll get caught if he does something bad—or it pays him to be good—he's too timid to be bad—or afraid of losing his reputation. He's good, but he's utterly selfish in his goodness.

The way to test real goodness in a man is to see what kind of a fellow he would be if there was never any danger of getting caught. What would you be like if you knew that you could get away with most anything? What would you do if you were sure of never being found out? That's the true test of morality.

There's a lot more to being moral than just behaving right. Being moral has to do with a man's spirit—with a man's relation to God. In fact, a man's relation to God is infinitely more important than his relationship to his fellow man.

Back of real morality is spirituality. Morality is between man and man—spirituality is between God and man. A moral man is not necessarily spiritual, but a spiritual man will be moral. The spiritual man is the key. Spirituality is the root of which morality is the fruit.

The trouble with much of our morality is that it has been cut from its roots. Man is concerned only with his relations with other men, and that concern is primarily selfish.

A man acts right in order to be looked up to, in order to guard his reputation, in order to be credited with his goodness. He's good so he can get ahead. Even his goodness is dictated by the tyrant of self.

When a man's morality never reaches beyond that low level, God is not pleased with it. He is displeased with it! Goodness for the sake of self-advancement is abominable to God. It is worse than badness, because it is masquerade—hypocrisy—deceit.

The goodness that really counts before God and man, that has depth and finish to it, is that which reflects the glory of God. The man whose moral living flows out of devotion to Christ is the true Christian.

"The LORD sees not as man sees; man looks on the outward appearance, but the LORD looks on the heart" (1 Sam. 16:7).

Grace

Have you ever seriously considered grace . . . the grace of God? If you understand but slightly the significance of God's grace, it can revitalize your life!

God's grace is inexhaustible! You can't use it up—wear it out! It is like the air you breathe: no matter how much you take in, or how often, or how many breathe at the same time, there is always plenty left.

161

It is *sufficient* for any need in your life! Don't let this slip by too easily! That means that God's provision for you anticipates way ahead, and more than covers any need you may have . . . whether material or spiritual.

It is *immediate* in its availability. Like the air, God's grace surrounds you, waiting to be let in. The split second you admit your need—open your life—it floods your soul with immeasurable supply.

Like sound waves: the air is full of them, but you've got to tune in on your radio to hear the music. You miss God's grace because you do not tune in. Really, no attitude in life is more stupid than to refuse to tune in on God.

God's grace is *constant!* It has no variable element in it. He is "the same yesterday, today and forever." He never changes, You can depend on God—always—anytime.

God's grace is *continuous!* It never stops. It is always there, right at the door of your heart, flowing, pushing, wooing, waiting . . . for you to let it in.

It is *all-forgiving!* This is the supreme expression of God's grace. "Christ died for our sins according to the Scriptures." In the cross, God revealed the infinity of His love. God's grace forgives all sin—on the basis of His Son's sacrifice on the cross.

All but one! It cannot cover the sin of refusal! Refuse to receive God's grace—it will not help you. Any more than the air will help you if you refuse to breathe . . . anymore than you can hear the radio program if you refuse to tune in.

God's grace is *free!* What an understatement! You can't earn it—you can't deserve it. If you earn it—if you are worthy of it—it is not grace. In fact grace means this—"unmerited favor." This is the key! Some men miss the point—in their pride, they try to earn God's favor.

One man refused the gospel on the grounds that it was free!

In his puffed-up self-reliance he dismissed it with these words: "I believe in paying my way. I don't need anyone's help." His false self-sufficiency was his greatest enemy. Actually it was stubborn pride! Wonder whom he pays for the air he breathes—and how much?

"As thy day, so shall thy strength be." "Where sin abounds, grace much more abounds." "My God will supply every need of yours according to his riches in glory in Christ Jesus." That's grace. Receive it!

What Are You Becoming?

It's not what you are! It's what you are becoming that really matters!

Life is never static! Life is motion—a way—a walk. Each man is going some place—becoming someone. Day by day you are becoming yourself.

In this sense, life is a perpetual crisis! Each choice—each decision makes a difference . . .

Because what you do today—now—in the next five minutes . . . what you think—what you say . . . all goes into what you are becoming. Every minute is a crisis for you. You're on your way—somewhere—to being someone!

Either you are moving upward or you are moving downward. It all depends on your direction, which way you are facing.

Direction means everything! If you are going in the wrong direction, each step carries you further from what you ought to be—what you really want to be.

Either you are becoming more and more what you want to be—and less and less what you abhor—or you are becoming less and less what you want to be and more and more the kind of a person you dislike.

The difference between a Christian man and a non-Christian is simply a matter of 180 degrees. The Christian man faces God—the non-Christian has his back to God.

At the moment there may not seem to be much difference. Their conduct may seem much the same—the non-Christian living pretty much as good a life as the Christian.

But as they progress, the difference becomes wider and wider. The Christian is walking toward God—the non-Christian away from God. Each step takes them farther apart—each man nearer the way he is facing.

That is why the "secular" attitude is diabolical. It is so subtle, so quiet, so smoothly regular and natural. But it is godless . . . men can live good lives without God . . . they do!

Ultimately, however, this wrong direction leads to destruction. The man who deliberately turns his back on God leaves God out of his plans and out of his life, but is doomed in the long run. He's walking away from God—farther and farther. He may walk too far . . .

Conversion means an about face. It's just a matter of 180 degrees. Turning back toward God. Then each step—each day leads to Him.

"Repent therefore, and turn again, that your sins may be blotted out . . ." (Acts 3:19).

Salt

"They're the salt of the earth," a man says about people he respects. It's a compliment . . . but why? Ever thought about its derivation?

Salt has many admirable faculties. Someone has pointed out that men have discovered more than 14,000 uses for it: It's a preservative—it keeps food from spoiling. It's seasoning—it brings out the flavor. It makes objects float—keeps them from sinking. It stimulates thirst.

"Ye are the salt of the earth," Jesus said of His disciples. Real Christianity works like a preservative in society. It slows down the decay and corruption. The benefits we take for granted were the by-product of the Bible: public schools, hospitals, welfare agencies, high status of women and children.

And there are still many places in the world (even in America) where the church is taking the initiative in these matters . . . areas that would still be without these benefits except for the pioneering world mission of the church.

A certain midwest town outlawed churches in its incorporation. The town drew riffraff like flies. Finally decent people refused to live there. The founding fathers had to relent—request churches to be established in order to save their town. Imagine your city—any city—without the church.

Faith seasons life too . . . brings out the flavor . . . keeps it from being drab and dull and monotonous. So many men are bored with life. They've had their fill of the best the world has to offer.

They've seen everything, heard everything, tried everything . . . and they're just plain fed-up with it all. Life has lost its luster and fragrance.

Real Christianity makes life palatable and delectable. It brings out the best in life. It seasons life—gives it flavor and tang!

Any number of men would have been sunk but for Christianity. Circumstances had almost overwhelmed them. In their extremity they turned to God. He lifted them up and out—put them on their feet. Faith floats men.

True discipleship creates thirst. The reason some men are indifferent to Christianity is that they have never seen it demonstrated. No one has given them an appetite for it. There's a quality about a real Christian that makes a man thirsty for God and righteousness.

The most effective Christian witness is a life that makes men seek for an explanation and find the answer in Jesus Christ. True devotion is contagious. Men want Christ—when they see what He can do for another.

One thing more: salt can gag too! Some Christians keep shoving their point of view down others' throats. They drive men from God—alienate them from the church. The Christian man should be careful—and wise in his efforts to win men to Christ. "Walk in wisdom toward them. . . ."

"Let your speech always be gracious, seasoned with salt . . ." (Col. 4:6).

Heart of Christian Faith

Some men think of Christianity only on the horizontal plane: man's relation to his fellow man. It's just a matter of morals and ethics.

But this is to miss the point entirely! Because ethics is the product of Christianity, not the process whereby a man becomes Christian.

Such thinking stops with Jesus as Teacher.

He was a Teacher—the greatest in history . . . but if Jesus is nothing more than a Teacher to a man, that man has not begun to grasp what Jesus taught.

For everything He said pointed up two basic matters: man's

alienation from God by sin and Jesus' purpose to reconcile man to God by the sacrifice of Himself.

In Jesus' teaching the issue was not horizontal but vertical. Not man's broken relationship with man, but man's separation from God.

He spoke of a vicious malady: a malignancy in the human heart that defiled man. Jesus made it quite clear that this was the root of man's trouble, and He had come into the world to do something about it!

In short, He had come to be a Savior, not simply a Teacher. His teaching was in order that men might realize their need of Him as Savior.

The Sermon on the Mount for example (as well as the Ten Commandments), was designed to serve a purpose much like a mirror. Man on looking into the perfect law of God would see his sinfulness and turn to Christ for help.

Any man who takes seriously the Sermon on the Mount will be led to despair if he takes Jesus only as Teacher. Because it is utterly beyond man's ability to fulfill. Only a Christ-enabled man can begin to live up to Jesus' ethics.

There's a subtle snare in the Jesus-as-Teacher line. If He is only Teacher (nothing more), it is relatively easy to keep Him at arm's length so to speak. One can take an academic interest in what He says and let it go at that.

Ironically to follow this line is actually to repudiate Jesus as Teacher for it "takes or leaves" the teaching depending on a man's feeling. He's in the questionable spot of honoring Jesus as Teacher while at the same time refusing to go along with all that He taught.

The heart and core of Jesus' message was His death. He came to die as a ransom for sin—to redeem man. He was the "Lamb of God, who takes away the sin of the world."

To reject this is to reject the Teacher who taught it!

This is central in Christian faith: man is a sinner . . . Christ has the only adequate solution. He is the Savior!

"The Son of man came to seek and to save the lost . . ." (Luke 19:10).

Technological Faith

A fantastic instrument perfected by the General Electric Company is an accurate and practical illustration of a down-to-earth principle of the Christian faith.

It's an electronic device called the "Co-Pilot." In case of an enemy attack the pilot of an interceptor makes a few rapid adjustments and thereby turns the controls of his plane over to the instrument.

From that moment the "Co-Pilot" takes over. It guides the plane to the target—intercepts the attacker—locks on target—fires the guns—and wings away from the target out of danger. And the pilot may never see the target!

Think of it. What a strange experience for a man to have. He gets in his plane to intercept an enemy. When the proper reading shows on his instrument panel, he makes a few rapid adjustments and takes his hands off.

He hears the guns fire, feels the plane wing away from the target, but he never sees the enemy. How does he know the enemy has been shot down? Because he has implicit faith in the instrument!

This is rather a crude illustration of the operation of spiritual law under God.

The Christian man makes some adjustments in his life,

adjustments that are clearly suggested in the Bible. From that moment he can have the confidence that God is leading and directing the affairs of his life.

Not because he feels like God is directing. Not because he has some sort of an emotional experience, but because he knows that God can be trusted. His confidence is not in his awareness of God. His trust is in the promise of God!

It probably isn't the easiest thing in the world for a pilot to learn to trust the complete control of his plane to the "co-pilot." Until he learns confidence, he is tempted over and over to clutch the controls—take over and fly his way.

But by experience he learns the device can be trusted. His confidence is not in his own awareness or feeling about the matter. He just knows the instrument can be trusted.

So the Christian man learns confidence in God by turning the controls of his life over. Of course, he's tempted to take them back, tempted to trust his feelings instead of God's promise. But gradually he learns that God can be trusted implicitly. Then he begins to live.

"Trust in the LORD with all your heart and do not rely on your own insight. In all your ways acknowledge him, and he will make straight your paths" (Prov. 3:5, 6).

Picture to Ponder

During the next Thanksgiving season take a look at a picture that has burned and etched itself permanently into my heart. Though not a pleasant one—perhaps even shocking— may it give a divine perspective.

Picture a large mansion set in the midst of lovely formal

gardens with expansive green lawns. A fabulous place—it has everything: colonnades, towering roof, picture windows, large rooms, rich furnishings, expensive carpeting, lavish decor!

The larder is something to behold: walk-in freezer lined with whole beefs and hams and lambs. Ice cream by the gallon—all flavors. Tons of frozen vegetables—juices—fish and poultry.

Fertile soil smiles with food for man and beast. A herd of purebred cattle give gallons of rich milk twice daily. The scene is one of luxury—opulence—and comfort . . . almost complete self-sufficiency. And surrounding it all a large stone wall.

Outside that wall, on every side as far as the eye can see, there is filth—disease—malnutrition—starvation—death. Indescribable misery and suffering everywhere. Men, women, and children living in poverty: wretched, hopeless!

On occasion the mansion people come outside . . . to see how "the other half lives." But nauseated by what they see and smell, they retreat to the comfort of their walls.

If possible they try to forget what lies outside. If the scene persists, they reason this way: "There's so much suffering out there. What we have would hardly be a drop in the bucket, so why even start to do anything!"

If we could see as God sees, something like that would greet our eyes! America, a land of opulence, luxury, and comfort . . . surrounded by a world of suffering and misery? . . .

Millions born into the world—living—dying without even knowing the feeling of a full stomach or a roof over their heads or clothes enough to keep warm or adequate medication for pain and disease!

Of course there are Americans who care, who are doing

something. Some are doing all they can. But others are unconcerned. Closing their eyes and ears to the misery of the world, they grumble at the slightest provocation. Living in their solid comfort, they don't even take time to thank God for their multitude blessings!

And God looks down and waits for America (not her government or a Marshall Plan) but the people themselves . . . all of them . . . to be thankful enough to soften their hearts, to loosen their death-like grip on possessions and try somehow, to the point of some sacrifice at least, to begin to do something!

"As you did it unto one of the least of these my brethren, you did it to me . . ." (Jesus Christ).

Point of Christmas

There is supreme reassurance in Christmas as a man faces a new year!

Christmas commemorates an event—the greatest event in history. This reminds us that Christian hope rests, not in ideas or ethics or theology, but in objective events in history. This is the thing that validates Christian faith: it is founded on solid fact, not on theory or speculation!

There are many qualities about this fact of Christmas that set it apart from all other historical events! The birth of Christ was unique in history. Nothing else like it ever happened!

It was unique in its anticipation. Hundreds of years before it happened there were scores of specific predictions concerning it: How He would be born. Where He would be born. His name, etc. It is mathematically impossible for these specific predictions to be coincidental. Their fulfillment testifies irrefutably to this event as divine!

Christ's birth was unique in its plan. Never before or since has a virgin conceived and borne a child. This was to be the "sign" according to Isaiah 700 years earlier. This was God's way of entering into human affairs to do for man what he could not do for himself.

And it was unique in its purpose! All others are born to live. Jesus Christ was born to die! His supreme purpose in coming into the world was to lay down His life as the sacrifice for sin.

The cross was not an interruption—not an unfortunate, unexpected, undesired, and premature end to an otherwise glorious life. On the contrary, the cross was the goal, the objective, the realization of God's purpose in history. He came to die on a cross! The "Lamb of God, who takes away sin. . . ."

This is why this event is so uniquely significant in history. Why Christmas holds such genuine reassurance in an inflammable world at the turn of the year. The birth—life—death—and resurrection of Jesus Christ were in order to redeem man. They were God's redemptive acts within history!

There is an immediacy—a relevancy about these redemptive acts of God in Christ. They are practical. They work now—today! They make it possible for a man to begin each new year as though he had not had a failure or a blunder or a fault or a sin in the previous year.

A man can start each year with a clean slate! All the past can be under the fabulous grace of God—covered by the sacrifice of Jesus Christ. Man's sin and error are forever forgotten by God when man turns to Christ in confession and surrender!

This is the glorious—the incredible—the phenomenal fact behind the Christmas event. Jesus Christ came into the world to save sinners. And He really does. If a man will turn to Him—let Him come into his heart.

"Glory to God—peace on earth among men of good will. . ."

Partnership With God

Harry B. Bullis, once Chairman of the Board, General Mills, Inc., said that God was his senior partner! In a feature article Mr. Bullis once told of the large and central place of prayer in his life.

From childhood he learned that time alone with God is never wasted! His sharpest wisdom—clearest direction—had been given him by God.

He never faced a major—or a minor—decision without bringing God into it by prayer. He lived this way most of his life . . . and he attributed his success to this practice.

We are reminded of the incredibly heavy decision President Eisenhower faced during the war in Europe.

The decision concerned the schedule for D-Day. President Eisenhower told how desperately he desired someone with whom he could counsel, realizing what a cosmic tragedy it would be should he settle on the wrong day for the big push.

But to whom could he turn? He was himself top command.

There was One to whom he could go! And he did! He spent time with God in prayer. He got direction—made the decision. The rightness of it has since been confirmed!

Big men do not hesitate to acknowledge their dependence

on God! The little man is the one who refuses to admit this need. Little men—with little souls! They issue their declaration of independence from God. Their lives show it!

It would be impossible to measure the broken lives, the failures, the defeats, the wrecked homes, the whipped men and women, the multiplied tragedies that could have been avoided had men known God—prayed to Him!

This is what America needs—in business and industry, in government, in education, in the professions, in the home . . . men who know God—who have a "speaking acquaintance" with Him—who take time to pray!

This is in fact—America at its best.

"Ask, and it will be given you; seek, and you will find; knock, and it will be opened to you" (Jesus Christ).

Contrast

I heard the story of a church in South Korea. It came first-hand through a friend who had been in the Orient. It's one of the most amazing incidents to come out of that little country.

Membership of the church after the Korean war consisted entirely of refugees . . . men and women driven from their homes by the war . . . weary—hungry—exhausted people who had been forced to leave everything behind.

The first thing they did in South Korea was to gather for worship—establish a church. Having no building they met outside until they could get a tent. They'd been meeting this way for a year.

When the call came for an offering to help other refugees, the church took up a collection . . . a thank offering.

Because none of them had any money, they gave their jewelry and everything else of value they possessed. When the gifts were turned into cash, the offering amounted to eight thousand dollars!

Eight thousand dollars from one congregation of Korean Christians—all of them refugees!

When asked the reason for the incredible offering, their explanation was this: They had come to South Korea with nothing. They had been able to escape from their homes with what they could wear and carry.

Though they had arrived with nothing, they were still alive! God had taken care of them, provided for their needs for a full year.

The best way to show their gratitude to God was to give Him everything of value they possessed—begin the second year from scratch.

This story came on the heels of an experience I had in trying to collect a little money for the local Y.M.C.A. There were six men on the list given to me. Two out of the six responded!

They worked in comfortable, modern offices in Hollywood. They were professional men—successful—prosperous—enjoying the unparalleled life of an American citizen.

Not only did they not give to the Y, they were quite irritated that they should be bothered by these fund-raising campaigns.

What a startling—staggering—humiliating contrast: Korean refugees giving everything in gratitude to God . . . strong—comfortable—prosperous Americans complaining about giving! God pity us if we don't wake up from this selfish, slothful, complacent, godless indifference to the needs of humanity!

"To whom much is given—much shall surely be required . . !"

Order of Faith

There's a logical order to faith that makes it practical—down-to-earth—relevant. When this order is disregarded or inverted, it reduces faith to a foolish thing subject to reproach and ridicule.

The logical order—the divine sequence—is fact—faith—feeling! Fact comes first, then faith in the facts. Feeling is the effect.

Men get it turned around. Some put feeling first. They pin their faith to their feelings. God and His Word are not the objects of faith . . . how they feel about things is. Consequently their faith is at the mercy of feeling.

When they feel low—discouraged—depressed—faith takes a tailspin. They find themselves in a vicious spiral. Depending on feelings to bolster feelings they sink into the pit of despair.

You can't depend on your feelings! They are erratic—transient—subject to what you eat—the weather—how much rest you get—traffic—the way things go on the job. Feelings are deceptive—capricious—vulnerable.

Your feelings about God may change. God Himself does not! A man may feel Godforsaken, but he's not! God says, "I will never leave you or forsake you." That's God's promise. He stands behind it. Don't believe your feelings . . . believe God!

Some put faith first—before fact. They have faith in their faith. But faith in faith is nonsense! Faith in and of itself is

176

nothing! Faith must rest in something—someone . . . and faith is worthwhile depending on the trustworthiness of that in which it rests.

Faith is valid—or null and void—according to the dependability of its object. Invest your money in a poor business, no matter how much faith you have, you lose your money if it fails. There is nothing wrong with your faith. It's the business that blows up.

You don't make a thing true by believing it! That's sheer delusion! If it's not true or dependable, faith won't change the fact!

Christians get faith-centered—treat faith as though it had a power all its own. They struggle to achieve faith. It doesn't come that way. You don't get faith by trying! Faith comes naturally when you cultivate a trustworthy object.

Get to know a trustworthy person—you don't have to force yourself to trust him. You do! The better you know him, the greater your confidence in him. The key to faith is knowing the one in whom faith centers.

Christian faith centers in the fact of Jesus Christ! Get to know Him—you'll have faith in Him. You can depend on that! Don't fuss with faith. Get acquainted with Christ. His promises are true. His integrity guarantees them!

"Faith comes from what is heard, and what is heard comes by the preaching of Christ" (Rom. 10:17).

Problem of Little Men

On a trip to the east coast: Washington D.C. and New York City—meeting many new friends among businessmen, industrialists, professionals, and government officials, a strong conviction gripped me—sank indelibly into mind!

It was this: the real basic distinction between men—the difference that matters—is not between goodness and badness so much as it is between littleness and bigness!

Rarely do you run into a really bad man in these circles of business, industry, professions, and government. They're good men by and large . . .

But you meet so many small men! Not small in stature, but men who think little, talk little, plan little. Like eagles staked to the ground there's no soar to them. Ceiling is zero, and their horizons are pulled in to the hub.

Not that these men are selfish. (Some of course are.) But it's just that they're preoccupied most of the time with their own little bailiwick. They don't allow their minds to stretch and breathe. They don't think—they just rearrange their prejudices.

They're looking at life through a microscope, never a telescope . . . or if they do look at life through a telescope, they look through the wrong end. The only time they get excited about world affairs is when they impinge directly on their own lives.

These little men are indifferent to problems other than their own. They have no concern for those things that do not hold a personal reference. They refuse to be bothered!

Here lies the tragedy of the little man—his unavailability. He is needed but unavailable! Needed by his community—his nation—the world . . . and he doesn't see beyond the four walls of his miserable little existence!

He excuses himself by pleading "too busy." But the interesting and significant thing is that the man who is really busy achieving things is the man who is always available!

It's the little man—busy doing nothing—who is never available!

In this desperately crucial, convulsive time, unavailability is a terrible sin. The times demand big men. Not men who are big shots . . . they're useless . . . but men who are big in heart and mind. Great men! Large-souled men!

Men with a vision, whose feet are on the ground but whose eyes are on the far horizon. Far-sighted, selfless men. Men with a goal! Men whose hearts God has touched. Men committed, dedicated to God and His holy, high purposes! Men of integrity!

Some men are good—good for nothing! Don't let yourself be that! "Present your bodies as a living sacrifice, holy and acceptable to God, which is your spiritual worship" (Rom. 12:1).

The Fruitful Life

There are two basic attitudes a man may have in life: One, the gambler . . . the other, the investor. One the "slot machine" attitude . . . the other, investment.

Some men look at life like a slot machine: They put in as little as possible—expect to get out as much as they can.

Such a man goes through life never giving himself, never really putting anything into it. And he's always expecting the break . . . expecting to hit the jackpot!

He usually envies and resents the man at the top—figures he had all the breaks! It never occurs to him that generally men make the top by dint of hard work—struggle—sacrifice.

In this spirit he complains that things never break right for him. The reason he gets no place is not his fault. It's always the fault of someone else or something else. He himself is never to blame.

The tragedy in this outlook is that it never pays off actually! Someday the fellow wakes up to discover—even with a few breaks—that though he hits the jackpot a few times, in the long run he's put more in than he'll ever get out!

Yet pitiful little men go through life with a chip on their shoulder, begrudging everyone who succeeds. They never give a man credit for his achievement, and never blame themselves for getting nowhere! Quick to make excuses for themselves, they never excuse others.

Little puffed-up tyrants—mouthing sour grapes at everyone who drives a better car—wears finer clothes—lives in a nicer home. Poor little men spending their lives at a slot machine—putting in nickels—dreaming of the jack pot!

A wise man treats life differently, realizes it operates according to the laws of legitimate investment. First concern is soundness! Investing in a questionable pursuit because it promises exorbitant returns, borders dangerously on the slot-machine philosophy. The first consideration is investing life productively.

The next thing to remember is that one receives in proportion to what he invests. The more he puts in—the more he gets out! He receives in ratio to his giving. The man who puts in the most is bound to get out the most. This is fundamental!

Of course some men get to the top by accident. This is the exception! Most men at the top paid the price—they risked, sacrificed, made the struggle of sweat—disappointment—defeat . . . plowed through to victory! The pay-off—success!

"Do not be deceived; God is not mocked, for whatever a man sows, that he will also reap" (Gal. 6:7).

"He who seeks his life shall lose it—he who loses his life shall save it" (Jesus Christ).

Strategy for Efficiency

The pressure of these days demands that you men practice the strategy of a daily quiet time. A time when you shut the door on everything else—and get in close with God for a brief period.

Nothing will settle your day—give you a high outlook—a sane perspective—like the practice of setting aside a period in the day for quiet meditation, for God.

Hard-headed businessmen are apt to think this impractical or nebulous or ethereal. Definitely not! Fact is, nothing can be more utilitarian in your business day than this strategy.

Take for example a glass filled with muddy water. Let the glass sit quietly awhile—watch the mud and sediment settle to the bottom. The water is clear as crystal . . . if you give it time and quiet.

Keep the glass stirred up—the water remains muddy and congested.

Your life is like that! It can get muddy—stirred up—confused under the pressure of circumstances. Your thinking is distorted—foggy—fuzzy—dull. You can't see issues clearly—objectively.

You get encircled by things: phones jangling, typewriters

clicking, decisions clamoring—jumping over one another—demanding action. Head buzzing—about to burst . . .

Shut the door and clear your desk—figuratively at least. Better still, stuff everything into a drawer for thirty minutes. Act as though there is nothing to do. Sit quiet, relax, let the chair hold you up.

Then listen to God . . .

Of course that's the key! It's not enough just to be quiet. You've got to be quiet intelligently. You don't want a mental vacuum. You want your mind and heart to be occupied with God—His Word.

Read a portion from the Bible: Psalm 1 or 23 or 37:1–7. Then think about these divine promises.

Talk the situation over with the Lord in prayer. Don't be concerned with prayer language. Talk to Him as you would a partner who has a deep interest in the business.

You'll get the bulge on your confusion in a hurry. Issues will take their proper proportions. You will be able to attack your work with a clear head—decisively—solidly.

"They who wait for the LORD shall renew their strength, they shall mount up with wings as eagles, they shall run and not be weary, they shall walk and not faint" (Isa. 40:31).

The Law of Life

One of the striking things about the writings of the apostle Paul in the New Testament is the way he uses the word "law" when speaking of certain moral and spiritual principles.

He never used words carelessly. To study his writing in the

Greek is to appreciate how meticulous he was in the use of words that would convey accurate meaning.

The brilliant apostle understood that there were certain laws that govern life in the moral and spiritual sense—just as there are laws that govern life in the physical sense.

These "natural" laws of life are unlike man-made laws. For man-made laws are arbitrary . . . they are different from city to city, state to state, country to country. Whereas civil and criminal laws differ from place to place, the natural laws of God are the same everywhere!

For example, the laws of music, health, chemistry, engineering, physics are the same in Los Angeles or New York or Paris or Berlin or Tokyo or Shanghai.

Furthermore, man-made laws do not punish the transgressor unless power of enforcement is present. But when a man breaks natural law, punishment is certain . . . although it may not be immediate! For God's law in nature has in it the seeds of its own retribution!

A man may exceed the speed limit and escape without penalty because no officer is present . . . but if he takes poison it will kill him! He may steal and not be caught, but if he disregards the law of gravity, and jumps into space, he will plunge to his destruction.

Somehow there is a peculiar quirk in men's thinking so that they can appreciate the natural physical laws such as gravity . . . but they live as though there were no spiritual and moral laws, as though a man could do anything and get away with it in this realm!

There is a "law of sin and death" says Paul, which is absolute—immutable—inexorable. To sin is to die. "The wages of sin is death." One can no more sin and escape . . . than he can take poison and escape!

This is as true of a nation as an individual: "Sin is a reproach to any people." History confirms the truth of this law of sin and death.

But although one cannot break a natural law and get away with it, he can bring into operation a higher law to offset it. Men discovered the laws of aerodynamics—submitted to them—obeyed them . . . and men fly without fear of the law of gravitation.

So God, even though man had sinned, even though man is dead in his sins, brought into play a higher law to counterbalance this law of sin and death. Paul calls it "the law of the Spirit of life in Christ Jesus."

Any man who will obey this higher law—the law of life in Christ—will be "set free from the law of sin and death." That is why Jesus Christ Himself—His cross—His resurrection—is the only answer to the sin problem.

"The wages of sin is death, but the free gift of God is eternal life" (Rom. 6:23).

Every Man Needs Christ!

One very illuminating fact about human nature is its unwillingness to admit need. Yet this admission of need is the one thing that qualifies a man to receive the grace of God.

On the surface it sounds rather strong and manly not to acknowledge need for divine aid, but get to the bottom of it and you discover it is in reality pride—ego—that keeps a man from admitting it!

Pascal wrote: "There are two classes of men in the world, the righteous—who know themselves to be sinners . . . and the rest—sinners who think themselves to be righteous."

The whole point of the Bible—both Old and New Testaments . . . the whole point of Jesus Christ—Peter and Paul . . . is that every man is a sinner—without exception! Every man is under the penalty, the condemnation of sin . . . under the "wrath of God."

But some men refuse to admit it. They insist they are not sinners. Actually what they're doing is contradicting the Bible. The Old and New Testaments—Jesus Christ—Peter and Paul . . . all are wrong!

These are they who are sinners but "think themselves righteous." That is pride! And pride is the root sin. Out of pride comes all sin!

Ego that sets itself against God, that refuses to acknowledge about itself what God says to be true, that remains wilfully blind to the light. Out of this festering ego comes all misery, woe, war, sin! That is the inevitable outcome when man sets his will against God!

Study that brand pride in the light of the cross and you will appreciate how utterly obnoxious, how abhorrent, how abominable it is! The matchless Son of God said He came to earth for one purpose: "to save sinners." He laid down His life on the cross, the only adequate remedy for sin. So He claimed . . .

And pride calls Him a liar, implies He need not have died. If man can save himself—lift himself up "by his own bootstraps"—then Christ died in vain. His cross was wasted effort—unnecessary—superfluous!

But man cannot! This is the distilled essence of the Bible!

Man has sinned—every man—no exception! You! I! All! But this is not the end of the story! There is a stupendous sequel . . .

God loves man, even though man sins. In the person of His Son . . . in the fact of the cross God provides absolution—complete and thorough pardon—justification—eternal life! It is ours for the taking.

On one condition: that we admit our need, confess our sin, take His proffered gift . . . in humility receive His grace!

"Since all have sinned and fall short of the glory of God, they are justified by his grace as a gift, through the redemption which is in Christ Jesus" (Rom. 3:23–24).

Balance

To understand himself a man must recognize a three-dimensional pull in his life: inward, outward, upward!

To be a whole man is to have each of these satisfied. Personal precision and efficiency come when the three are in proper balance and tension.

Disregard any one—neglect it—the result is distortion in the life. A man is a caricature of himself.

Inward pull is the demand for individuality. Man craves to be something in and of himself. When his dignity is violated—his inherent worth ignored—he begins to revolt within himself.

He will endure indignities for awhile, and allow himself to be handled like chattel, but pressure builds up until either there is recognition or an explosion!

In the economy of God each man is of inestimable worth. This is the foundation of democracy—the American way.

When any system tampers with this fundamental priceless-ness of man, making him a pawn or tool, that system seals its doom.

Opposing the inward pull is one as basic as individuality, which keeps individuality from becoming anarchy . . . it is the demand for togetherness.

Man was not meant to be alone! Though of ultimate value in himself, yet he is never really himself until he "belongs" to a society.

The worst off in a mental hospital is the one who has retreated into a shell—utterly isolated and insulated from the rest of the world. Man alone is an aberration!

Any system that violates the unity of mankind is doomed to failure as well.

Most important is the vertical pull in a man's life. Man was built to be in touch with God. This dimension gives meaning and direction to the other two. This dimension makes life make sense! A man is never himself until God comes first!

The danger men face is in emphasizing one pull at the expense or complete exclusion of the others. They promote man's unity at the sacrifice of his dignity . . . and quite often ignore the vertical relationship altogether.

Here's where Jesus Christ is the answer! He establishes fellowship! This is to be right within—with others—and with God. Christian fellowship nurtures all three dimensions in a man. Hence it brings poise, dignity, unity, efficiency.

In reconciling men to God, Christ reconciles them to each other . . . and by giving the peace of God within, reconciles a man to himself.

"That which we have seen and heard, we proclaim also to you, so that you may have fellowship with us; and our fellowship is with the Father and with his Son, Jesus Christ" (1 John 1:3).

Forgiven and Forgotten

One thing that makes it difficult for a man to make a new start is the sense of failure—defeat—and sin that dogs him just at the time he is most seriously attempting the new beginning.

The past over which he has no control, moves in—clouds up—and bogs down a man's aims and ambitions for the future. You can fight this, but at best it cuts way in on a man's determination.

This is one reason why Christian faith is real and relevant! In one sense, this is the whole point of Christian faith!

This is where the grace of God comes in. Or to put it another way, the forgetfulness of God! God is infinite and unchangeable in all His attributes: love, mercy, justice, goodness . . . and in His grace too! His grace is inexhaustible. He is infinite and unchangeable in His forgetfulness!

This is the workable, practical aspect of Christianity. It prevents the failure and sin of the past from laying a dead hand on the hopes and aspirations of the future!

Like a vicious malignancy, guilt lodges in a man's heart, infects his whole being with poison that can often be felt physically. It vitiates a man's strength, his drive, his incentive. It eats out his vitality and undermines his plans.

It robs him of efficiency, takes the edge off of his power, cuts into his productivity, slows him down in every way.

Many times it shames him into quitting or giving up, and not trying a new start.

There is a cure for this creeping cancer of guilt. One cure! It is the grace of God in the sacrifice of Jesus Christ on the cross. This is "the power of God unto salvation. . ." This is the one and only solution!

It literally cures this malady. It actually removes the guilt by divine surgery in the soul. The infection is purged—and destroyed.

The Bible abounds in God's promises that guarantee this grace to every man who wishes to avail himself of it. God will not force it on a man. He must ask for it, receive it freely, without coercion.

God's grace blots out the sin. It washes and cleanses, forgives, buries it, forgets it forever, removes it as far as the east is from the west. It transforms the man! God's grace is regenerative!

This is the incomparable truth of the gospel. God so loved the world that He gave His Son. The Son so loved that He gave His life on the cross. Forgiveness—cleansing—renewal are the free gifts of God and Christ to any man who wants them! No strings! No gimmicks! Just grace! Try it!

"If we confess our sins, he is faithful and just, and will forgive our sins and cleanse us from all unrighteousness" (1 John 1:9).

Master Motive

One of the things that makes a man great, that makes him a large soul, that makes him productive, is strong incentive . . . some dominant drive in his life that demands—and gets—the best there is in him!

There are men who do not have this! Their lives are directionless, fruitless, unproductive. They live little! They come and go without notice. They never add a thing to life . . . just poor—little—unnoticed men. The world is no better because they've been here!

This is doubly tragic! No man need be a little man. There is room for—demand for—bigness all down the line.

Bigness never depends on where a man works, but what he's working for. It does not depend on how much money he makes, but how he uses what he has. There are some mighty big men in little places . . . and they transform those little places—make them big, important, indispensable.

By the same token there are plenty of little men in big places . . . and they degrade and desecrate their position with their puny little selves!

Bigness depends on a man's master motive . . . on the dominant drive in his life. It depends on what he's living for!

Generally this master motive can take two directions: inward or outward. It can turn in to the man himself, or out to others.

Inevitably when the master motive turns in on self it is destructive! When a man lives for himself, he ends up all by himself. His soul dries up, decays, rots inside. Ultimately he even gets fed up with himself!

But when the insistent incentive is away from self, when a man lives for others, when he gives up his right to himself, he opens the door to growth in every direction. This is where bigness—"large-soulness"—begins!

Selfishness, self-centeredness, is at the bottom of all our

troubles: personal, family, industrial, national, international. Out of the malignant, cancerous root of self issue the problems that plague man.

Being subtle and sophisticated makes no difference. Smooth or cultured selfishness is just as loathsome. It holds just as much putrefaction as the bull-headed, obvious kind. Only when men let go of themselves will they begin to find the road to a cure.

That's why Christ died on a cross!

"He died for all, that those who live might live no longer for themselves but for him who for their sake died and was raised" (2 Cor. 5:15). Jesus said, "He who seeks his life shall lose it. He who loses his life for my sake will find it."

What Are You Becoming?

As men grow old, they turn one of three ways . . . sour, bitter, or mellow! What you are now is important, but what you are becoming is exceedingly more important!

What makes the difference in a man's becoming is not so much what he does, as it is how he takes the things done to him!

Life plays a lot of crazy tricks on men. They seem crazy simply because a man doesn't distinguish between the end and the process. In the process some things don't make sense.

Like looking at a building under construction. Scraps of lumber, brick, metal, dirt, debris . . . and scaffolding. It's not a pretty sight—there's no apparent design. To the unpracticed eye, just a mess—without rhyme or reason.

But the building is not crazy, it's unfinished—incomplete! You're looking at the process, not the end product. Wait until the job's done, and you'll get the whole picture. The scaffolding and stuff had a purpose!

So in the process of becoming, funny things happen to men. Things that appear utterly unreasonable—ridiculous—purposeless. Failure, defeat, tragedy, injustice . . . seem insurmountable at times—don't make sense. But wait! The end's not yet? . . .

But if a man treats these "detours" of life as the end, he'll turn bitter—sour. He'll curdle inside. His soul will shrivel up like a prune. He will lose his spontaneity, incentive, drive! The pay-off is cynicism!

It's these things that separate the men from the boys! It's these shadows, detours, clouds, difficulties, defeats that build into the man strength, courage, flexibility, maturity.

Jesus Christ does this for men! He gives man a perspective on life. Keeps him from being swallowed up in the process. Equips him to meet every exigency, face every difficulty, take it in stride . . . see in it the stuff, the raw material from which character, maturity, manhood is made.

Actually the Christian man has no fear of age. Life doesn't "peter out" for him when he's walking with Christ! Life is one grand becoming . . . and when the Christian leaves his body behind, he doesn't stop . . . that's not the end by a long shot. He goes right on to unspeakable glory!

In Christ, whatever hits a man, no matter how hard or how unexpected, it simply makes him a better man—solid, strong, real, mellow!

"The way of the wicked is like deep darkness . . . but the path of the righteous is like the light of dawn, which shines brighter and brighter until full day" (Prov. 4:18).

Sanctuary in Industry

Men in business, in industry, in the professions, are finding that the pressure is increasing these days . . . and there doesn't seem to be any sign of a let-up.

Forces from every angle seem designed to break men . . . conspire to confuse . . . to drain a man of strength, incentive, drive . . . until he feels like throwing in the towel at times.

Have you ever really tried God in such circumstances? Have you given Him an opportunity to prove His relevance in difficult days? Are you really practicing Christianity, or is your religion just talk?

Take for example a very good friend of mine. He's general manager of a manufacturing company, having the usual trouble with getting supplies, with consumer demands, and government orders.

Prayer plays an important part in his business! To him it is a direct wire to the best and wisest counsel available. When he gets tied up on a production problem, he lifts the receiver of prayer and makes contact with his heavenly Father. His office becomes a sanctuary for a few moments . . .

He goes back to his job with renewed strength, with clearer insight, and sharper vision. He actually receives wisdom from God. He actually experiences divine strength. He settles down, moves in on his problem, and solves it! The job's done and he's a better man . . . because of prayer!

This is not a child at play talking . . . this is a man in business, in the midst of production schedules, tough competition, incredible pressures. This is fast-moving, 20th-century industry . . . and prayer is an integral part of it!

You're missing a big bet when you fail to let God into your daily affairs this way. The Christian man who takes God seriously in all the details of life will always have the edge on his difficulties.

Not that a man "uses" God for his own ends! That's not the point! This friend sees it just the opposite way. He isn't interested in "using" God; he turns it around and lets God use him. God is not just a "trouble shooter"—He's the Lord!

He's running the factory to the glory of God, living for the Lord the best he knows how. He doesn't always succeed; he gets discouraged at times, but he keeps at it, determined the business will be run God's way.

God is honoring that man in business! God delights in this! "Those who honor me I will honor" (1 Sam. 2:30).

Face it, man! You need God—and He is more than willing to lift you, to guide you, to help you! But He will not force Himself on you! He waits for you to come to Him—admit your need—ask for His grace. Why not let prayer have its place?

Slavery—Your Choice!

What things dominate your life? Examine yourself at this point. You'll find this to be an index to your true self! You'll find also that it is a key to your effectiveness—or ineffectiveness—as a man!

Dominating influences work in two directions in a man's life! They may enslave . . . they may emancipate! Some have an inexorable, binding influence . . . some work to free—liberate a man!

The important thing to realize is that each man is responsible for what dominates him! I am responsible for what dominates me. You are responsible for what dominates you! If I am a slave to myself—I am to blame . . . I yielded to myself.

It is entirely up to the man whether his life will be dominated by a tyrant . . . or by an emancipator! Each man is free to choose. God built freedom into the very framework of man's nature. Man can enlarge that freedom—or forfeit it—depending on his choices.

Think of the men in your experience who have yielded to tyrants. Perhaps the tyrant is a habit—not in itself bad—but it has a narrowing, confining, limiting influence in the life. There are so many puny, picayune, paltry things that make slaves of men.

One man complained bitterly on the plane bound for Spokane. We had to wait on the ground a prolonged period for a minor check-up. He couldn't smoke—made a terrible fuss. What a pity!

It's really tragic—big men slaves of little things. They've got to have a smoke—got to have a drink—got to swear—got to play the horses—got to gamble. They deny it . . . but they can't stop!

Then there are those who yield to a social circle—let themselves become tools of selfish interests. Their goal becomes "keeping up with the Joneses." No mind of their own, they follow the crowd—sheep-like.

The things you read, the company you keep, the places you go, your conversation, the way you spend your leisure . . . these limit or expand your life. They are tyrants or friends, depending on the way you yield.

There is one tremendous exception! There is one Master

who grandly frees! He is in fact the only One who is able to free a man from all tyrants. Jesus Christ—of course!

Yield to His mastery in your life—He breaks the bands of all other tyrants. If you want Him to! He will never free you beyond what you desire!

Whatever you yield to becomes the control factor in your life. It's up to you! Yield to a tyrant, the chains begin to bind until the last link is forged. You're trapped! Yield to Jesus Christ, maximum freedom is yours!

"Do you not know that if you yield yourselves to any one as obedient slaves, you are slaves" (Rom. 6:16).

Crucible of Suffering

One of the questions that perplexes men is the old, old one—"Why do good people suffer?"

Sometimes it takes a more cynical tone—"How can you believe in a God of love with all this human suffering?" Behind this of course is the idea that God is responsible for the misery.

Which is simply not true! God does not cause suffering! Sin is the root cause of suffering. All human woe and misery flow out of man's rejection of God . . . out of man's rebellion, his sin!

If man were not free, he would not be man . . . he would be a machine—a robot—an automaton. God made man free. That's what makes him a man! That's part of the "image of God" in him—his free and sovereign will!

Man abuses that freedom in turning from God. That choice opens the floodgates of misery, pain, suffering. That choice is at the bottom of all that plagues humanity! "The wages of sin is death. . . ." That is an irrevocable law, built into the very fabric of life!

The only way that God could put a stop to suffering would be to destroy that which causes suffering—human nature. Man's lust and passion and greed give birth to misery.

Men cry out for peace. They want God to stop war, yet they reject the Prince of Peace—repudiate God's will for their lives. They crave peace, but refuse the way to peace. Sheer stupidity!

But there's another, better explanation! In the divine economy misery becomes a sacramental thing to the man who follows God—to the righteous man. God utilizes suffering to man's benefit. Taken God's way, it has healing, strengthening, maturing qualities.

As rivers become crooked, dodging difficulties . . . as roads stay narrow and crooked, taking the line of least resistance, so man's character is dwarfed, stilted, ingrown, shallow, apart from suffering.

The crooked river—the narrow road—cannot carry heavy traffic. And the life that is void of hardship, the life that is free from travail and sorrow, is not qualified to carry the loads. Great men are those who have mellowed and deepened and matured through stress and strain. This is the stuff of which leaders are made!

This is preeminently true of the greatest life lived. It was said of Jesus Christ, ". . . He became perfect through the things which he suffered." The only perfect man who ever lived, suffered most . . . for you and me!

God does not cause suffering! But He uses it—channels it—controls it! He turns tragedy into triumph for His people. "More than conquerors . . ."

"Do not be surprised at the fiery ordeal which comes upon you to prove you . . . but rejoice . . ." (1 Peter 4:12).

The Power of God Unto Salvation

Some years ago a very unusual movie appeared on television! It was the story of a man—a little man—who received the power to work miracles.

His power was almost unlimited. He could change anything—anything with one exception. He could not change human nature. He could change people's circumstances, but he could not change people.

He could provide money without limit. He could heal disease. He could transport a man from London to San Francisco in a flash of a second. There was nothing he could not do . . . except change human nature.

Being a little man he was rather confused, fearful, timid about this strange miracle-working power with which he had been endowed. So he sought the counsel of wiser men: a banker, a businessman, a visionary, a judge.

The businessman wanted to form a corporation—get a monopoly on this little man's miracles. The banker—well, he was greatly alarmed at this power to pull money out of thin air . . . good money at that! After all, where would bankers be if everybody could have all the money he needed—or wanted . . . just at the drop of a hat. It was a rather frightful prospect.

The visionary, quite unselfishly, suggested that the little man usher in a "golden age" . . . rid the world of disease, pain, work . . . nothing to do but just . . . well, just "love one another."

But what of the medical profession? What was to become of doctors should this little man by a twist of the wrist rid the world of sickness and pestilence? Another rather grim picture!

The judge was frankly outspoken. This miracle-working business was an outrage! It would upset the status quo, interfere with his plans, disrupt everything. He vetoed the idea of a "golden age." Tried in fact to kill the miracle worker.

Give people everything they want: wealth, health, happiness . . . and not change the people themselves? Well, it just wouldn't work! Fantastic? To be sure! But put yourself in the little man's place. What would you do?

Fiction of course! But how revealing, how illuminating! Nothing will work but some power that will change human nature itself, rid it of selfishness, greed, lust. Nothing is solved as long as these remain in men's hearts.

And there's only one power that can do that! Jesus Christ—and He alone—is adequate to save humanity! He can change a man's heart—any man's!

That's the whole point of the gospel! It has power—unlimited power—to solve the fundamental problem! If we would only give Christ a chance to prove it! If men would only listen to Him, obey Him, trust Him!

"I am not ashamed of the gospel: it is the power of God for salvation to every one who has faith"—Apostle Paul (Rom. 1:16).

Root of Liberty

One of the "modern" ideas (it is fast becoming obsolete) that has infected much of twentieth-century thinking, is the idea that moral and spiritual law curtails man's freedom.

Ridiculing moral law by labelling it "mid-victorian," "old fashioned," primitive, prudish . . . "modern" man struggled to set himself free . . . and freedom to him meant the elimination of moral and spiritual restraints.

He became inflamed with the delusion that a man's freedom consisted in doing as he pleased . . . without "taboos"— "blue laws" and other obsolete standards that cut into his "liberty."

Forgotten was the life principle that the Bible writers knew well. Divine law is not something superimposed on life from without . . . it is fundamentally rooted in human nature as created by God.

Divine law is not an obstacle to happiness . . . it is on the contrary a directive, a guide to true happiness. Man's greatest freedom—maximum liberty—lies within the bounds of God's law.

There are practical illustrations almost without number. Consider the champion golfer. He plays the game so easily. He became champion, not by ignoring the rules of good golf, but by studying them—obeying them—practicing until they became second nature to him.

A great concert pianist. He mastered the laws of music. He became a slave to those laws. Hours and hours, years and years of sacrificial practice, until he made those laws second nature in himself. It looks so easy . . . but it is the product of solid discipline!

Or take an Olympic star. Effortlessly he glides over the cinder track to new world's records. But that easy glide is the result of years of learning the laws of the track—obeying them—becoming a slave to them.

Watch a master surgeon. He did not become that by disregarding law. He gave himself to the laws of surgery and medicine until finally he expressed unconsciously—in his mind—his body—his fingers—the laws of surgery.

No man ever became great doing as he pleased. Little men do as they please—little nobodies! Great men submit themselves to the laws governing the realm of their greatness!

Burned into the very fabric, the warp and woof of history, is this strong confirmation . . . the man, the nation, the people who obey God rise to unbelievable heights. Those that disregard God—His law—are doomed!

This is the tremendous truth, man! Take God seriously and obey Him. You will find yourself, your highest happiness, maximum productivity, and largest freedom.

"Do not be deceived; God is not mocked; for whatever a man sows, that he will also reap" (Gal. 6:7).

The Case for Intolerance

It's profitable to think through what we mean by tolerance. Because if we're not eternally vigilant, tolerance becomes spineless, sentimental, and willy-nilly acquiescence to anything and everything—without any stand for principle whatever!

History confirms America as a nation with Christian ideals. From her birth, the Bible, the gospel, prayer, and Jesus Christ have been central in the establishment of her great documents and traditions.

Included in the principles on which our nation was founded is that of religious freedom. Which means every man is free to worship God after the dictates of his conscience. Religion cannot be legislated!

But religious freedom does not mean we ought to repudiate the Christian faith which gave birth to America! Religious freedom does not mean we must apologize for being Christian—and forget our Christian heritage!

Yet there are those who enjoy this freedom America provides, and at the same time use this principle of religious freedom to undermine the faith that made that freedom possible!

And whenever the historic Christian faith is talked about or promoted publicly there are those who set up the hue and cry of intolerance. As though it is unpardonable to propagate this faith that made America possible!

Mention Jesus Christ in a public gathering and some will cry out that this shows discrimination. Even to close a prayer "in the name of Jesus Christ" in some circles in America is to risk the criticism of being "intolerant."

And the tragedy is that many Christian people are sucked in by this round-robin reasoning: either all religious traditions get equal public attention . . . or none at all! What kind of logic is that in a nation founded by Christians?

The result is that many who reject Christian faith (and all faith) use the freedom Christian faith guarantees them to make insidious attacks on it! In the name of tolerance great *intolerance* is practiced!

Let anyone speak with conviction about Christianity and these people cry out: "Intolerant!" "Narrow!" "Bigot!" Separation of church and state has been reduced to separation of God from government, education, and public life!

Let's square with this business of intolerance! Tolerance certainly does not mean that we stand for nothing at all! It does not mean a man has no convictions. Let tolerance become that and freedom is lost to the most abusive intolerance of all! *America does not believe in sheer religious anarchy!*

Men may live in America and worship God however they please! But let them recognize that the privilege to do so rises out of a deep Christian faith.

America stands for Christian love—not compromise . . . tolerance—not anarchy. The surest guarantee that this freedom will continue is to be intolerant of attacks on its spiritual foundation!

Prudent Planning

How much are you really worth? Actually how rich are you? Personal inventory is wise, too . . . as well as business inventory.

You don't have to be reminded that these are tempestuous, explosive, unpredictable days. What do you have that an unexpected disaster could not take away from you in a matter of minutes?

How do you measure your real worth . . . your true wealth?

Are you counting on the false security of a bank account, good health, an automobile, things? They can be taken from you in a flash!

Is it conceivable that intelligent and prudent men are blind enough to equate life with possessions? Wise in other matters, are you so misguided as to measure your personal worth in terms of things?

What would happen to your values, should a nuclear attack blast your city apart? "No danger," you say? Perhaps not! Maybe it's utterly remote . . . and maybe it's just around the corner! No one really knows. Why be an ostrich—bury your head—pretend that there's no danger?

Brilliant men most closely in touch with scientific and military affairs are fearful. There's no room for smugness and complacency now!

Not that we are to be governed by fear! Fear is paralyzing . . . at best it is weak motivation, but we ought to be guided by astute, discerning, prudent judgment!

How much would you be worth if a catastrophe were to dissolve your possessions? That's the way to measure your essential worth.

Possessions are not unimportant, but they are secondary! They don't come first . . . or if they do, the man who gives them that place is a fool of fools.

God comes first! Actually you're worth exactly what you hold in your heart for God. Do you love God? You love to eat, drink, wear fine clothes, live in a nice house, drive a good car. But do you love God?

Or are things your god? Do you possess your possessions, or do they possess you? Are you master of your things, or do things master you? Therein lies the index to your intrinsic value.

"Life does not consist in the abundance of things a man possesseth. What shall it profit a man if he gain the whole world—and lose his own soul? Seek ye first the kingdom of God and its righteousness. . ."

Jesus Christ gave us the truth about life. May we see it— alter our lives by it. Wisdom begins at this point . . . obedience to Jesus Christ!

The Strategy of Depth

How do you measure a life? What scale is the standard for evaluating a man? What dimensions apply?

Do you measure it like a string—by length? Are the years a man occupies this earth the clue to his effectiveness? Methuselah lived 969 years, which is about all that can be said for him. Jesus Christ was 33 when He was crucified. There's more to life than length of years. Some men do more in twelve months than others do in a decade.

Do you measure life like a board, by breadth? Is the index to a man's life how much he has extended himself in influence? In this powermad world is this the final arbiter of greatness? Is life measured in terms of domination?

Alexander the Great ruled the world . . . wept because there was no more to conquer . . . cursed his lack of self-control. Hitler ran rough-shod over Europe and held millions in his iron grip. So Mussolini! So Stalin! But no man in his right mind would want to emulate any of them!

When Jesus Christ died on the cross, He had at the outside 120 faithful followers. Breadth is not an accurate index to greatness in men!

Is the height? Is greatness measured by how high a man goes? How much money he makes . . . how popular . . . how famous . . . how great prestige?

A man is worth a cool $9 million. He jumps from the twelfth floor of a building and smashes to a miserable death on the pavement! One of Hollywood's brightest stars becomes a pitiful crumpled heap on her bathroom floor . . . sleeping pills!

Periodicals are filled with stories of men and women who reach the pinnacle in a blaze of glory, only to fizzle out. They've hit the top . . . but they're bored—fed-up—frustrated—exhausted!

You don't measure life by height—breadth—length! There is another dimension that gives the clue.

In the Bible a man is measured by depth. Man is like a tree.

Everything depends on his roots! When storms strike—the roots are the thing!

"Blessed is the man who walks not in the counsel of the wicked, nor stands in the way of sinners, nor sits in the seat of scoffers; but his delight is in the law of the LORD. . . . He is like a tree planted" (Ps. 1:1–3).

Or man is like a building. Everything depends on his foundation! The best superstructure is useless if the foundation can't stand the stress and strain!

"Every one then who hears these words of mine and does them will be like a wise man who built his house upon the rock. . . . Every one who hears these words and does not do them will be like a foolish man who built his house upon the sand . . . and great was the fall of it"—Jesus Christ (Matt. 7:24–27).

The Christian View of Law

There are two ways of looking at law: from the standpoint of the letter and from the standpoint of the spirit. The latter is the Christian viewpoint—the former is distinctly not!

Keeping the letter of the law may be done, while at the same time the law in fact is broken . . . because its intent is missed entirely. Keeping the letter of the law is a device of crooks. The Christian man is bound by the spirit of the law always!

In essence that is the point of the Sermon on the Mount. Sadly enough there are men, even Christian men, who insist the Sermon on the Mount is not practical—not workable in our day. This is contrary to the truth!

Take Jesus' closing words: "Everyone who hears these words

of mine and does them will be like a wise man. . . . And everyone who hears these words of mine and does not do them will be like a foolish man. . .”

This does not sound that He intended for men to receive His message as some impractical, unworkable ideal for a far-off day . . . some Utopian of an "other-world" kingdom. . . .

He expected men to hear and do . . . to obey—now! This was a challenge to action, not an encouragement to apathy or inaction or preoccupation with some future, ethereal condition.

The Sermon on the Mount, an amplification of the Ten Commandments, emphasizes inner obedience, rather than outward observance! That is the key to Christian morality.

There is something infinitely more important than mere dogged, slavish adherence to the letter of the law! Motivation is more basic than conduct. Spirituality is the root of morality—the life blood of ethics.

Christ went beyond murder to a more basic evil—anger! He delved more deeply than the overt act of adultery—condemned lust in the heart. That is where sin is born—in the heart . . . that's where obedience begins!

Not only does Jesus Christ expect the Christian man to live this way, He made provision for it! Not only does He insist Christian righteousness "exceed the righteousness of Scribes and Pharisees" (which was rigid adherence to the letter), He makes it possible for the Christian man actually to fulfill this requirement!

It is possible in the Holy Spirit. The fruit of the Spirit is the fulfillment of the law's intent. His righteousness is manifest in the life of that man whose life He fills, in whose heart the Spirit is in control. This is Christ's desire: men filled with His Spirit—submissive to His control!

". . . that the just requirement of the law might be fulfilled in us, who walk not according to the flesh but according to the Spirit" (Rom. 8:4).

The Amazing Book

As Sir Walter Scott, the great English author, lay dying, he requested his son to bring him "the book." The son asked, "Which book?" To which Scott replied, "There is only one book—the Bible!"

Such reverence for the Bible was not the superstitious, sentimental, mouthing of an ignoramus. It was the conviction of a man of letters—a brilliant scholar—a literary genius.

What an amazing phenomenon—the Bible! Written by more than forty different writers, living in entirely different cultures, over a period of 1500 years, in at least three languages, about many different subjects: history, hygiene, physics, astronomy, jurisprudence, ethics, philosophy, psychology, etc. . . . virtually a library—yet regarded as one book.

Knowledge of the Bible reveals that the sixty-six books that comprise it are concerned with one central theme—redemption . . . that every part ties into every other part to form an organic unity. It leaves but one sound and reasonable conclusion: The Book is God-directed—protected—inspired.

Who could measure the impact, should Americans take a serious interest in the Bible—read it daily—obey it! Let's begin with you—with me!

"Blessed is the man . . . whose delight is in the law of the LORD . . ." (Ps. 1:2).